SUCCESS
IS NOT AN
ACCIDENT

SUCCESS IS NOT AN ACCIDENT

Change Your Choices
Choices
←→
Change Your Life

TOMMY
NEWBERRY

AMERICA'S SUCCESS COACH®

Published by
Looking Glass Books
730 Sycamore Street
Decatur, Georgia   30030

Manufactured in the United States of America

Library of Congress Card Number 96-095186

ISBN 1-886669-09-0

America's Success Coach and The 1% Club are registered
trademarks of Tommy Newberry Coaching Systems, Inc.

Cover photography by Doug Jarrett
Cover design by Paulette Livers Lambert

Also by Tommy Newberry

*366 Days of Wisdom & Inspiration
with America's Success Coach®*

Getting Results

High Speed Success

Peak Performance for Christ

The Secret Place

Talk Yourself Into Success

Vital Time

Acknowledgments

Writing a book is a monumental project. Although the author's name appears on the cover, it requires a team of dedicated people behind the scenes to make the undertaking a success. As I've learned over the years, few significant accomplishments can ever be completed alone, and this book is no exception. While it would be virtually impossible for me to list all the people who have influenced me and contributed to *Success Is Not An Accident,* I do want to recognize a special few who helped make this book possible.

First, let me thank the graduates of my personal coaching programs for their many suggestions, observations, and insights. In particular, special thanks to the founding members of The 1% Club®: Dave Armento, Jeff Bak, David Bland, Bruce Boring, Phil Coleman, Tyler Edgarton, Tom Elias, Emery Ellinger, Scott Goodman, Matt Hawkins, Quill Healey, Bill Holman, Marty Jones, John McIntyre, Chris Morocco, and Paul Raulet. Your pioneering spirit, encouragement, and constructive feedback have been invaluable to me and to the writing of this book. Thanks for believing in me.

I am thankful that my own thinking has been positively influenced by so many wise and insightful writers and speakers such as Brian Tracy, John Maxwell, Charles Swindoll, Jim Rohn, Stephen Covey, Mark Victor Hansen, Norman Vincent Peale, Paul Pilzer, Earl Nightingale, and Robert Schuller to name just a few.

Thank you to Dick Parker at Looking Glass Books for your guidance, patience, and sound advice. I really enjoyed working with you.

I am especially grateful to my special assistant, Kimberly Zwaagstra who read and re-read and constantly re-typed my early drafts while juggling 1,001 other pressing projects. Thanks for all your help.

Thanks to my parents, whose unconditional love and encouragement prepared me to chart my own course and do wise, wonderful, and grand things with my life. As the years go by, my appreciation grows for the example you have set and the wisdom you have passed down.

Boundless thanks to my terrific wife, Kristin, who never let me forget how much she believed in me as I worked through this manuscript as though I were moonlighting. Your patience will be rewarded.

Foremost, I want to thank God for my special combination of talents, gifts, and life experiences, as well as the inspiration, and creativity that allowed this book to become a reality.

This book is lovingly dedicated
to my Mom and Dad;
my sisters, Cindy, Suzanne, Jenny, and Beth;
my son, Ty;
and to my wonderful wife, Kristin.

Contents

Introduction

I am writing this book at a time when certain politicians, with an assist from the media, continue to bombard Americans with the erroneous and disempowering message that *success* only happens to the "privileged or fortunate few." If you "happen to be successful," then it can simply be equated to winning the "lottery of life." These misleading words actually come out of the mouths of individuals positioned at the highest levels of our government. The truth is that success occurs in the lives of specific people for specific reasons. Success is not something that randomly happens to you; it is something that you make happen. There is no magic. It is not complex. If you will invest the time to find out what other people have done to be successful, and then begin doing the same things, you too, in due season, will achieve similar results. Ralph Waldo Emerson wrote, "Let him learn a prudence of a higher strain. Let him learn that everything in nature, even dust and feathers, go by law and not by luck. And that what he sows, he reaps."

Presenting success as a condition arrived at through luck only serves to promote government and those in power as the saviors for all our problems, thus creating a debilitating dependence on government to "make things fair." It also shifts the focus from admiring the successful to knocking the successful. You can view those who are more successful as role models or you can resent them. You can learn from them or be jealous of them. You can become wise or you can become bitter. You can waste valuable energy complaining or invest your talents and energy taking constructive action.

One has simply to take a glimpse around the globe to see the distress and destruction that has eventually caught up with those countries who penalized their achievers — who, in the name of fairness and compassion, brought down their successful few only to realize too late that they were demolishing the foundation.

A country can reach its full potential only through a political system that allows the greatest personal freedom to the individual. This freedom includes the opportunity, but not the compulsion, to exercise the virtues of personal initiative, self reliance, individual responsibility, resourcefulness, courage, perseverance, and personal excellence. An individual must be allowed to reap the fruit of his own efforts, and those who choose to skip the planting season must be taught at an early age that they have to forgo the fruit as well. Never should a government directly or indirectly reward or promote idleness, inefficiency, or mediocrity. All government incentives should encourage self-reliance, innovation, entrepreneurship, and personal excellence.

Nobody really wants to be mediocre or average. The seeds of greatness lie within us all. It is only when we stop believing that a better life is possible that we begin to settle for less, convincing ourselves that it just wasn't meant to be.

This book is written for those who look to themselves

and God as the solution to their problems and the path to an extraordinary life here on earth. Imagine trying to hit a dart board in a room with no lights on. Even in the dark you would eventually hit the board, and if you continued for long enough you would probably hit a bull's eye. But if you turned on the lights, gathered a large supply of darts, and invested ample time to practice, you would significantly reduce the time it would take to hit the dart board. And when you finally hit the bull's eye people would call you lucky. But you weren't lucky. You were just willing to do more things to ensure that you hit the bull's eye.

This book was designed to help you identify the factors within your control that will increase the odds that you hit the bull's eye in your own journey through life.

The seven lessons in this book follow the same curriculum I have been using in my one-on-one coaching for many years. Over time, I have upgraded and refined my coaching programs in response to much appreciated feedback from my clients. I compiled the curriculum in book form with encouragement from my personal coaching graduates so that its content may be made available to a wider audience.

Together, the seven lessons represent a complete system for managing yourself and your life more effectively. When you begin to incorporate the principles from each lesson into your daily life, you will begin to report the same positive results my clients have repeatedly experienced. I know this is true. I have seen it happen over and over again with each of my clients. It still amazes me, though. I've seen the system in this book work for both male and female clients. I've seen it work for my clients fresh out of college and those earning high six-figure, and in several cases, seven-figure incomes. I have seen this system work for my single clients, and I have watched it work for my clients who are married with families.

To be fair, I do not want to imply that my system has

worked equally well for all of my clients. Very few people have applied this system in exactly the same way and with the equivalent level of discipline and diligence. I can assure you, however, that the life management system you are about to learn will work for you to the exact degree that you apply its principles consistently in your day to day life. This book, in essence, contains a formula that has been proven to generate positive, predictable results.

I *encourage* you to blend your personality with my system to create your own unique system. I must constantly remind you that the principles of effective living are non-negotiable. Universal principles work in our lives whether we like them, understand them, or even know about them. I *encourage* you to put your personal slant on the ideas in this book, as long as you strictly abide by the principles. In other words, focus on the spirit of the law, rather than just the letter. The principles taught in each lesson are built upon the firm foundation of truth. The principles that underlie my system are not untested theories or my particular opinions. They are proven approaches or steps to enjoying and succeeding in the game of life.

I've observed throughout my life that when individuals stray from timeless principles, trouble and adversity of some kind are never far behind. You can observe this for yourself with children and adults alike. There are unwavering principles that govern each area of our lives as well as principles that govern our lives as a whole. When we attempt to bend, stretch, or otherwise pervert these principles, we set ourselves up for pain and regret in the long run. The most successful individuals who have ever lived have resisted the natural human tendency to make up their own little laws of life. Likewise, if you want to develop all the potential within you, you must avoid the trendy "principle of the day" mentality that has permeated our society.

The good news about universal principles is that they will always be there for you. No matter how often you abandon or slander them, they will still welcome you back like the prodigal son with open arms. You will, naturally, experience the repercussions of getting off track, but the right course is only a principle or two away.

The principles supporting each lesson in this book can be compared to the fundamentals in baseball. The baseball team that adheres to the fundamentals most consistently wins most consistently. It is really no mystery at all. When a team drifts into a slump, it is often described as playing "sloppy ball." This description simply means they have strayed from the fundamentals of winning baseball. Even a talent-packed team of superstars will stop winning consistently when they fail to execute the proper fundamentals. By refocusing on the fundamentals, individuals, as well as teams, break out of slumps.

View the lessons in this book as your playbook for successful living. This playbook describes the essential fundamentals for living an exceptional life. Putting these fundamental principles into practice consistently is the prerequisite for designing a life worth living. This playbook also includes a variety of drills or exercises that sharpen your understanding and application.

For the rest of *Success Is Not An Accident*, allow me to be *your* personal success coach. As I tell my clients, "My job is to help you get the most out of yourself. My goal is to help you reach your goals." Throughout each lesson in this book I will challenge you to be the best you can be. I've tried to write with an underlying tone of encouragement and accountability. Sometimes, like any good coach, I may appear overly blunt or even harsh. Don't take it personally. I just don't want to let you off the hook. I do not want to see you cheat yourself and your family out of the fruits of your full potential.

As you work through each lesson, you will find the most practical and usable ideas and methods for improving your performance that have ever been discovered or developed.

Throughout this book I will give you new information, new perspectives, new strategies, and new skills. I will break the complex into the simple. Sometimes, though, I won't be teaching you anything new. I'll just be reminding you of what must be done and exactly when you need to do it.

I truly hope you will implement the entire system laid out in this book. If you do, it will change your life forever. Each lesson is a component of the entire system. While you will make significant gains by applying only one or two lessons, you will amaze yourself and others if you put the complete system into action. When you fully integrate the system into every area of your life, you will experience a surge of confidence, competence, and unparalleled optimism for the future. The responsibility for implementation is all yours. I cannot do it for you.

This is not a book about living like most people live. You don't need a book to do that. It just happens by default. If you live your life like most people do, you will get what most people get. You will settle for what most people settle for. Here's a taste of "most people." Forty-nine percent of marriages now end in divorce. Eighty percent of people working today would rather be in another line of work. More than fifty percent of Americans are overweight. One out of three will get cancer while two out of five will suffer from heart disease. More than sixty percent of Americans, living in the richest, most abundant civilization in history, will retire with little or no savings, dependent on so-called "entitlements" for survival. If you want to lead an extraordinary life, find out what the ordinary do and don't do it. That is a simple but true formula. Remember, no one plans to become mediocre. Mediocrity is the result of no plan at all.

Finally, in writing this book, I hope to further my personal mission of positively impacting people's lives by teaching the timeless, proven principles of successful living. By writing this book, I do not claim to be superior in any way.

In fact, you probably have many natural talents and abilities that are greater than my own. I just have a burning desire to share the truth about success with others. These truths existed long before I came into this world and they will survive long after I have gone.

If you put into practice the principles that follow, you need not be surprised when you succeed. And if I fail to practice what I preach, then I need not be surprised with my failure. Success is in your hands. Just as Olympic athletes have coaches, I want to be your coach. I want you to become a world-class human being, someone who pulls out all the stops in each area of life.

About the Format

At a glance you will see that this book differs from most others you have read. Although ordinary type fills most of the left-hand pages, many of the right-hand pages contain diagrams, enlarged text, and drawings. The opening page to each lesson includes a rundown of benefits you'll get by incorporating the principles that follow, and a closing page offers assignments to incorporate the lessons into your daily life. The format is based on a super learning technique, which promotes more effective and efficient understanding and retention.

This book was designed not just to be read, but internalized. It will give you not just knowledge, but immediately usable strategies and techniques for living a balanced, significant, and impactful life. The information on the pages that follow can be the difference between an ordinary life and an *extraordinary* life.

Now, let's get started.

Lesson 1

Choose Success

Your success blesses others!

Develop a meaningful definition of success

Accept complete responsibility for your choices

Eliminate excuses

Become a doer

Tune in to prosperity

Success is not an accident! This is, without a doubt, the single most important lesson you must learn and really understand if you want to develop your full potential and enjoy all the success you were designed to enjoy. Success in life comes from one thing: *deciding* exactly what you want to accomplish and then deliberately *choosing to invest* the minutes and hours of your life doing only those things that move you in the direction of your goals. It's simple. It's the truth. And the moment you fully accept it, your life and the lives of those you love will never again be the same. Success, however you choose to define it, is absolutely predictable.

Get Clear on Success

Specifically, what does success mean to you? Answering this question is one of the first assignments I give my personal coaching clients. Investing the time and effort to define success in your own terms is one of the most helpful mental exercises you can undertake. Considering that my clients have enrolled in a program designed to accelerate their success, it only makes sense to first define the target, which in this case is elusive and often misunderstood. I assume that if you're reading this book you want to accelerate your progress as well. So consider the question of success for yourself.

What exactly does success mean to you?

I've observed that most people find it quite difficult to define success. But if you don't have a clear picture of success, how can you honestly pursue it or expect to achieve it? Success has been defined many times in all areas of literature. Success is the progressive realization of a worthy ideal...Success is the accomplishment of God's will in your life...Success is making the most of what you have...Success is who you become...Success is living your life in your own way...Success is a journey.

How do you define success? Do you equate it with

wealth? Do you believe you're successful if you have a lot of friends and social status? Do you think you're a success if you own a nice home, car, or other worthwhile possessions? Does power bring success, or is it the accomplishment of the next goal on your list that will finally usher in success? Maybe success is early retirement, or maybe it comes when all the kids have gone away to college.

Success, simply put, is an emotion we all want to experience. The problem is that most of us go through life borrowing someone else's definition of success!

Are you experiencing success right now? If you aren't, take some time to re-examine your concept of success. Where does your definition of success come from? Whose definition are you using? I've found that trying to distinguish between the words of achievement, happiness, and success to be a very helpful exercise in formulating your definition of success. Can you be a success without achieving anything? Can you be a high achiever without being successful? Can you be happy without also being a success? Maybe! Of course, this all depends on your definition. Is your definition reasonable and attainable? Do you require all areas of your life to be perfect before you allow yourself to experience success?

Be aware that the natural tendency is to mentally set an almost unreachable standard for success while simultaneously creating a definition for failure that is easy to meet. As a result, you may feel a lot less successful than is necessary. Creating a definition of success that allows you to experience the emotion of success often tends to promote even more and greater success in the future. Success breeds success. Once you have your new, constructive definition of success, allow some time to internalize it and really believe in it. You have to buy into it to get it working for you.

The most successful people in the world are those who have taken the time to figure out exactly who they want to become and what they want to achieve, and then invest the

5 criteria to help crystallize your unique definition of success

1. *Controllable: Make your definition within your control, not based on outside circumstances or other people.*

2. *Measurable: Make your definition quantifiable so that you can hold yourself accountable.*

3. *Perpetual: Formulate your definition so that you can satisfy your definition on a daily basis.*

4. *Personal: Choose your own definition, not a borrowed one.*

5. *Principle based: Establish your definition on absolute truths, not on subjective, timely or situational values.*

hours of their days in activities consistent with these ideals.

The unsuccessful are those who have no real direction in life. These people tend to "go with the flow," or drift in whichever direction the wind happens to be blowing. Their lives are controlled by circumstances and overflowing with excuses. Life, they claim, "has dealt them a bad hand," and they choose to fold.

Get over wanting things to be fair. A level playing field is a silly and unproductive fantasy as far as peak performance is concerned. It will never happen, nor should it. You can focus on reaching your goals or on the obstacles that stand in your way. Your choice will lead to accomplishment and progress or to frustration and alienation. Everybody has disadvantages, handicaps, weaknesses, and various other crosses to bear. A big part of life is learning how to transform your disadvantages into advantages. While directing your energy toward "making things fair" is often destructive and counterproductive, channeling your mental and physical energies toward the achievement of meaningful goals is a constructive investment of time. Consider that some people are naturally more intelligent than others. Some people are more creative than others. Some are born into poverty and some into wealth. Some receive great love and little else, while many others are given everything but love. Some people are considered "better looking" than others. Some people can run faster, jump higher, or hit a baseball farther than others. Some receive the best of educations and contribute little to the world, while others get little formal education yet leave a magnificent mark. Some have fast metabolisms while others must exercise twice as much just to keep pace. Some people are predisposed to migraines and sinus infections and others are not...and so on. This phenomenon is called life.

The truth is that life, if viewed as a card game, deals good hands, bad hands, and average hands. And whichever hand you receive, you must play! You can win with any hand and you can lose with any hand. It's *totally* up to you and how you play the game! Life is filled with champions who drew extremely poor hands, and with losers, who drew terrific hands. In life, unlike cards, you will

When you try to get something for nothing, you become nothing.

never be dealt a hand that cannot be turned into a winner. Success is for you and for anyone willing to take the initiative and pay the price. If you put into practice the principles outlined in each lesson of this book, you will be well equipped to do whatever it takes to turn your hand into a winner! Go for it!

Sow, Then Reap

Success is a planned outcome, not an accident. Success and failure are both absolutely predictable because they follow the natural and immutable Law of Sowing and Reaping. Simply stated, if you want to reap more rewards, you must sow more service, contribution, and value. Success in life is not based on *need*, but on *seed*. So you've got to become good at either planting in the springtime or begging in the fall.

The Bible says, "Do not be deceived; God is not mocked, for whatever a man sows, that he will also reap." Unfortunately, many Americans have been deceived, confused, tricked, and misled into believing they will not be held accountable for their choices and that they will miraculously harvest something other than what they planted. I call this the *big lie*. This dangerously popular distortion promotes mediocrity and underachievement. Consider the effort and expense Americans undertake to solve and cure diseases and social problems while they do very little, if anything, to avoid them. It is popular to treat the symptom of a problem, but it is often considered "insensitive" or "intolerant" to address the root causes. As a result, an attitude pervades in our society that denies that effects really do have causes. The truth is this: There are no exceptions to the law of causality. It is impartial and impersonal and it comes to us in a particular order — sow *then* reap. This God-given natural law was old when the pyramids were new. Like gravity, it works twenty-four hours a day, seven days a week, everywhere in the world, regardless of whether anyone has ever told you about it. It is simply impossible to harvest something that has not been sown, though many squander their entire lives attempting to do just this only to end up in frustration. Success is the effect generated by right thinking and right actions. Success, and failure for that matter, are not accidents, but consequences. **If you want to know what you sowed in the past, look around you and see what you're reaping today.** You begin your climb toward your full potential as a human being the moment you accept and absorb the truth that cause and consequence are inseparable.

The mark of a fully mature, mentally healthy individual is the acceptance of complete responsibility for one's life. When you accept total responsibility, you recognize that you are the cause of all your choices, decisions, and actions. When you are anchored in the reality of responsibility, you are far more likely to act in ways that will not later become causes of regret, frustration, or embarrassment. Life is a two-for-one deal. With every choice, you get a free consequence.

Everything Counts

Everything you do or fail to do counts. Every action has a consequence even if it isn't immediate. At this mo-

What are the likely consequences of each of these actions?

- *jumping off a building*
- *daily aerobic exercise*
- *watching two or more hours of TV daily*
- *reading one hour each day*
- *sitting in the sun without sunscreen*
- *investing 10 percent of your income*
- *using illicit drugs*
- *eating a diet of whole grains and fresh fruits and vegetables*
- *eating fried foods*
- *running in front of a speeding truck*
- *robbing a bank*
- *lying to your best friend*
- *studying hard in school*
- *smoking*
- *writing goals down*
- *drinking excessive alcohol*
- *drinking just a little alcohol*
- *drinking no alcohol*
- *studying parenting*
- *reading a book on marriage*
- *touching a hot stove*
- *studying successful people*
- *praying*
- *purchasing depreciating assets*
- *spending beyond your means*
- *waking up at 5 a.m.*
- *waking up at 7 a.m.*

Remember, when you make a choice, you also choose the consequence of that choice.

ment you are becoming more like the person you want to become or you are not! There is no neutrality. Several years ago I was watching a major league baseball game on TV when the base runner, Deion Sanders, attempted to steal second base but came up about two feet short from the bag as he slid. He immediately sprung to his feet and back tracked toward first base. Seconds later, when it became inevitable that he was going to be tagged out, Sanders put his hands together in the football time-out sign and yelled "time-out, time-out," to no avail, but with laughter from the fielder and the umpire. Sanders was tagged out. That is the way life is. Whether you're running the bases or pursuing your goals, there are no time-outs. The sooner you learn this lesson, the better.

Nobody can stop the ticking clock. If you try to call time-out, you will always be tagged out. What you do Friday night counts, just as what you do Sunday morning or Thursday afternoon counts. An extraordinary life is simply the accumulation of thousands of efforts, often unseen by others, that lead to the accomplishment of worthwhile goals. **You are rich with choice.** And your choices reveal who you really are. More than any other single factor, you are where you are today because of the choices you have made. You've made decisions about what to learn and what not to learn. You have made decisions about who to spend your time with and who not to spend your time with. You've made decisions to believe some things and not to believe others. You've made, or will have to make, decisions about who you will date, who you will marry and whether you will have children. You've made decisions to persevere and decisions to give up. You've made decisions on whether or not you will drink, smoke, or use drugs. You've made decisions on what you will eat or not eat. You've decided either to write down exciting goals for your life or to just wing it. You have made decisions to give in to fear and decisions to press on in the face of fear. You've made decisions to be the best and decisions to act like all the rest. Consider for a moment all of the decisions you've made in just the last three years. These choices are made daily, hourly, and minute to minute. Imagine having

> My father taught me that the only helping hand you're ever going to be able to rely on is at the end of your sleeve.
> — J.C. Watts

made a different choice in some key area. How might your life be different today?

What's Your Excuse?

I believe the slogan of the Paralympics says it all in the form of a question: What's Your Excuse? Often, questions are the best teachers because they prompt us to really think through an issue. When we're simply told something directly, we're more likely to smile politely and then let our thoughts drift to another subject. Questions can be captivating because we're conditioned to at least mentally answer the question. So ask yourself this question: "What is my excuse?" What does this question mean to you? What images does it evoke in your mind? As I ask myself, "What is my excuse?" I notice that my mind races to the aspects of my life that aren't quite like I want them to be. It reminds me of the excuses I've given others and the excuses I've silently told myself. It makes me laugh a little at myself and reminds me that while I was making excuses, others just like me were making progress. I remember the first time I heard the classic homework excuse, "My dog ate my homework" from a third-grade classmate who didn't even have a dog. The entire class, including the teacher, broke out in laughter. I don't remember whether the excuse was "successful," but I do remember the laughter and the combination embarrassed/proud expression on the face of my classmate. Looking back, I realize how appropriate and natural the laughter was. Excuses should be laughed at, not dignified as they often are today. Excuses and responsibility cannot coexist. If you have one, you cannot have the other. It's very easy to say, "I'm *not* responsible," and so hard to say, "I *am* responsible." If there is anything in your life that is not the way you want it to be, you and only you are responsible for changing it. Whether it's something big or small, you're still responsible, and each time you give an excuse you diminish your respect, your credibility, and your integrity in your own eyes as well as the eyes of others. Each time you make an excuse, you reinforce your propensity to make even more excuses in the future, and excuse making becomes a habit.

Whenever you act irresponsibly and feel the need to make excuses, your brain goes into overdrive, attempting to rationalize your lack of results. There appears to be a variety of *rational lies* for almost every occasion. Unless you make a commitment to the choice of excuse-free living, you'll always be able to find excuses. Some will be better than others, of course. These will become your favorite excuses which you'll carry with you at all times, because you never know when you might need them. Eventually they'll be passing out free excuses in our public schools.

The Excuse-Free Zone

Commit to making your home and office an *excuse-free zone*. If a situation arises that previously called for an excuse, substitute the words, "I am responsible," where the excuse used to go. Look only to yourself for the cause of your problems or lack. Whenever something doesn't work out the way you hoped, claim responsibility and ask your-

The Excuse Exploder

Whenever you think of an excuse, ask yourself if there has ever been anyone, anywhere who has been in similar circumstances and who has succeeded in spite of it. When you move beyond the whining and justifying, you'll find that the answer is almost always "yes." Somebody, somewhere has usually had it far worse than you and still succeeded. And you can succeed as well the moment you want a goal more than you want an excuse. Refuse to appoint yourself a victim. Victims don't have to take action. They're too busy dwelling on injustice and being bitter. Remember, you will always be able to come up with an eloquent excuse, but there are no excuses with a shelf life of more than 24 hours.

self, "What could I have done to avoid the problem?" Imagine yourself opening your refrigerator and taking out the orange juice. Following the instructions on the label, you begin to shake the carton vigorously only to have the cap fly off and orange juice spew all over you, the counters, the floor, and even a little on the ceiling. At this point, you have two options:

1. You can immediately blame the numskull who didn't screw the cap on after he used it and demand that he help you clean up or...

2. You can remind yourself, "This mess could have been avoided altogether if I had only checked the cap before I started shaking the carton. Of course, it would have been nice if the previous person had secured the cap, but the power to prevent this situation was in my hands."

Taking responsibility for your life is like being a good defensive driver. If your car is totaled in an accident, it won't provide much comfort to remind yourself that you had the green light. The question that will resonate in your mind is, "What could I have done to prevent this?"

Blaming the other driver won't help much either. It will only defer your attention from what you need to learn.

Stay empowered and in control by analyzing all unpleasant situations from the perspective of *what you can do to avoid their recurrence.*

Excuses are contagious, self-defeating bad habits. Where you find one person making an excuse, you'll find others infected with excusitis as well. You don't like to hear excuses from other people and they don't like to hear yours either! Stop excuses before they start by creating an environment conducive to success. Make it easy for yourself and others you depend on to succeed by **anticipating and eliminating all excuses in advance**. This is the true measure of how intensely you desire your goal.

The only thing more damaging to your success than making an excuse is making the same excuse twice. **Remember, there is never enough room for buts and bril-**

liance. You must make the choice. Do I want my Big But or do I want my goal? You may be thinking, "Yeah, but, in my particular situation things are different." Lose the "Yeahbuts..." as well. They've never helped you and they never will.

> High achievers are motivated by pleasurable outcomes. Underachievers are motivated by pleasurable methods.

Feelers and Doers

The world can be divided into feelers and doers. Feelers take action and initiative only when they feel like doing so. In other words, they feel their way into acting. If they don't feel like doing something that will advance their goals, they won't do it. If a feeler feels like exercising, he will. If he doesn't feel like exercising, he won't. If a feeler feels like watching television, he will. But if he feels like reading instead, he will choose to read. A feeler's decision-making ability is wired to his short-term emotional appetite. He is a prisoner of the desire for instant gratification, and naturally will suffer the long-term consequences of this short-term perspective. Feeling-driven thinking is shallow thinking. It lacks character, conviction, and maturity. Feeling-driven thinking is also a habit.

Doers, on the other hand, act their way into feeling. After determining what needs to be done, doers take action. They just do it. If they don't feel like taking action, they consider that emotion to be a distraction and take action in spite of it. They refuse to let their desire for short-term comfort divert them from their long-term goal.

You become a doer by making a definite and deliberate decision to do so. You become a feeler by default, by neglecting to consider this aspect of your character at all. In the absence of a definite decision to do otherwise, we are all prone to giving in to the worst side of human nature. We are all very likely to engage in actions that only produce immediate payback.

The alternative to a life restricted by feelings is a life unlimited by action. The antidote to a life of comfort and mediocrity is a life of character and courage. You can live a life of action and character by shifting your thinking from short term to long term. This means you must consider the long-term ramifications of every action you take or don't take. Ask, "If this act were to turn into a habit for me, would that be in my best long-term interests?" If the answer is "no" don't do it. Or you can ask, "How might this decision affect me 20 years from now?" Or you could ask, "How might this decision affect me 1,000 years from now?" That one should get you thinking.

The most important determiner of the quality of decisions we make is our perspective, or frame of reference, going in. If our time horizons are long, then we will likely reap the effects of wise choices. If our horizon is short, then we will inevitably suffer the negative consequences that correspond with short-term thinking.

Abundance or Survival?

You can walk up to the ocean of abundance with either a thimble or a tanker truck. Most people, unfortunately, choose the thimble, never even knowing that there was an alternative. God has poured an inexhaustible supply of abundance onto this earth ready for us to multiply it even further if we are willing to take the initiative. Most people do not seize the initiative simply because they have learned to think in terms of lack and survival rather than in terms of abundance and prosperity. This thinking pattern is often referred to as "poverty thinking" or a "scarcity mentality" and is characterized by a focus on how little there is versus how much there is. It is inherently pessimistic. Someone with a scarcity mindset is overly aware of what they *do not* want in life and unsure about what they *do* want. They have long mental lists of why things can't be done and why it is of no use to even try. "Why set a goal when you can not possibly achieve it?" is a typical response of these deficit thinkers. A scarcity mentality sends one into the survival mode where "just getting by" becomes the goal and, consequently, the ceiling. Of course, those suffering from a poverty mentality are seldom aware of it.

An abundance consciousness, on the other hand, is anchored in possibilities and huge thinking. There is a concentration on how and why things can be done. An abundance thinker dwells upon the opportunities that exist now as well as those that should exist. An abundance mentality precedes all extraordinary accomplishment, and it is your birthright. Watch out for the "A-word" and the "R-word." Get away from what you can *afford* and **focus on what you can earn** when you change your approach. Get away from what is *realistic* and **consider the seemingly impossible possibilities**. Stop asking what a good goal would be and start asking **what your most magnificent goal should and could be**.

No matter how prosperous your mindset is, it can be even more prosperous. Remember, **your success blesses others**. As you increase the quality and quantity of your service to others, your rewards increase as a natural consequence. As you become more prosperous in your thinking, you become like a formerly color blind child in a fabulous garden suddenly able to see the rich images that have been there all along. You can tune in to lack or you can tune in to prosperity. Again, it is your choice.

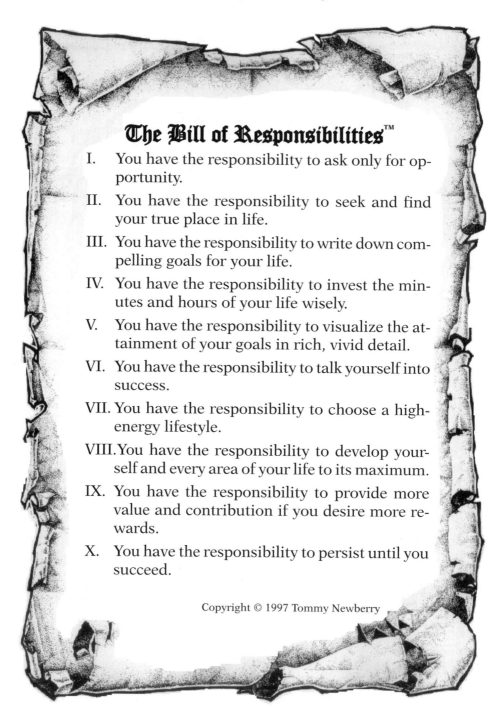

The Bill of Responsibilities™

I. You have the responsibility to ask only for opportunity.

II. You have the responsibility to seek and find your true place in life.

III. You have the responsibility to write down compelling goals for your life.

IV. You have the responsibility to invest the minutes and hours of your life wisely.

V. You have the responsibility to visualize the attainment of your goals in rich, vivid detail.

VI. You have the responsibility to talk yourself into success.

VII. You have the responsibility to choose a high-energy lifestyle.

VIII. You have the responsibility to develop yourself and every area of your life to its maximum.

IX. You have the responsibility to provide more value and contribution if you desire more rewards.

X. You have the responsibility to persist until you succeed.

Lesson 1
<u>*Assignments*</u>

1. Write out your personal definitions of success and failure.

2. Draw a line down the center of a piece of paper. On the left hand side, write down everything in your life that you can control, either partially or completely. In the right hand column, write down those aspects of your life over which you have absolutely no control.

3. Write out 20 of your positive characteristics.

4. Write out 20 of your past accomplishments.

5. Write out 20 of your greatest blessings.

6. Write out 20 blessings you expect to be grateful for 9 years from now.

7. Describe your ideal day in detail, from the moment you wake up until you drift to sleep. Include as many emotion-provoking details as possible.

Lesson 2

Choose Who You
Want to Become

_If you want your mission in life to become
a magnificent obsession, you have to constantly
remind yourself of that mission._

Choose who you want to become

Cultivate a deep sense of personal mission

Live more honestly, freely, and intuitively

Craft an inspiring personal mission statement

Align your goals with your purpose

efore you choose your goals, it is wise to first choose who you want to become. Throughout your life, you will be constantly changing and becoming someone new, either slightly or significantly different from the previous version. With each change you will move forward or slip back. For most people, change just happens. Change is considered an external event that occurs randomly and haphazardly, and there is very little that can be done about it. Most people unknowingly allow themselves to be shaped by their circumstances. But as James Allen wrote in *As A Man Thinketh*, "Circumstance does not make a man, it reveals him."

This is one of the most important laws of human nature ever discovered. Our circumstances are just a reflection of what is going on inside our private world of thoughts, feelings and beliefs. Human beings are really human becomings. **As we begin to change, our world changes with us.** As we become better, our lives become better. Changing circumstances requires that you first change yourself. To have it any other way is to have the cart before the horse.

Operating yourself for maximum performance requires deciding in advance how you want to change. You must make things happen rather than let things happen. You must make the shift from reactivity to proactivity.

In this lesson, I want to lead you and coach you through the process of creating your personal mission statement. I will share with you some of the exercises I assign to my clients as they develop their personal missions. Finally, I am going to give you a simple formula that will help you generate the first draft of your personal mission statement.

As human beings, we need a sense of purpose in our lives as much as we need food, water and oxygen. This sense of purpose provides meaning and significance to our lives. It makes us feel useful. It is a constant reminder that "my life matters." When you tap into the wellspring of your personal mission, you become more creative, energetic and

> *Today will take its place as a single tile in the mosaic of our finished lives — to either add to its beauty and harmony or detract from it in an undedicated, purposeless life.*
> **— Earl Nightingale**

passionate. You become totally absorbed in the pursuit of your goals, like a child at play. Emerson said, "According to the depth from which you draw your life, such is the depth of your accomplishment."

You have no greater responsibility than to determine what you were put here on earth to accomplish. Why do you exist? How do you want the world to be different because of your life? Generally, everyone shares a common purpose of learning, growing, and contributing. In this purpose we all must find our true place, our area of genius. Your true place is your unique path to learning, growing, and contributing. No matter how far you may have strayed from your true place, you can always find it again. Your true place is always waiting for you because no one but you can fill it. Every experience you have ever had, no matter how seemingly unrelated, can be utilized to your advantage in your true place.

When you arrive in your true place, you will know it. A sense of destiny will come over you as what you most love to do becomes what you do best. You will be in your area of genius. You will be spending your life in your own way, making the difference that only you are uniquely equipped to make. The more you experience your true place, the more you will be drawn to it. You will begin living more honestly, freely, and intuitively. The tinge of dissatisfaction, which only you knew existed, will disappear. You will enjoy invigorating surges of self-esteem as there is no longer a need to compare yourself with anyone else. You will be happier, healthier, and more prosperous.

While each of us has many different paths where we can do well, there is but one road to genius. For some, this area of

Do what you love and you'll stop being your own worst enemy.

genius will shake the entire world. For others, it will soothe just one tiny home. In either case, you will leave the world a better place.

With a deep sense of personal mission, you live from the inside out. This means that *who* you are triggers *what* you do. Your outer life honestly and accurately reflects your inner life in terms of values, priorities and principles.

Without a strong sense of purpose or mission, life is empty and devoid of true significance or long-term meaning. This type of existence is characterized by going through the motions, cynicism, pessimism, apathy, and ultimately, a life of mediocrity. It is a life that constantly needs to be filled up with things from the outside.

Sooner or later, everyone will be confronted from within with the question of whether his or her life is on purpose.

What sort of reputation do you want to have? For what qualities do you want to be known? Once you have made these decisions, goal setting and goal achieving become much easier.

A personal mission statement is a written articulation of exactly what type of person you ultimately want to become. It expresses your unique purpose for living. Your personal mission statement encourages you to change in a deliberate, preconceived direction. The process of constructing a personal mission statement forces you to seriously think through the vital areas of your life. Creating a personal mission statement requires reflection, introspection, and a considerable quantity of mental effort. For this reason, it is not an exercise that is appealing to the masses.

Once you have completed your personal mission statement, you will have a clear picture of the person you hope to become. This understanding, of course, dramatically increases the odds that you will actually become that person. A good mission statement clarifies what is allowable in your life. It helps you say "yes" to the right things and "no way" to the wrong things. It reminds you of what is true and false in your life.

A written mission statement is the bridge from intention to action. It shows who you want to become and, more importantly, *what* you are willing to do differently to become that person. Having a written personal mission statement is an outward sign that you have accepted complete responsibility for your life and your future.

When completed, your personal mission statement should act as your constitution. It should be the unifying element around which you organize the rest of your life. You should consider your goals to be laws that have already passed the constitutional test. You should also be very conservative in your interpretation of your personal constitution. Your integrity depends on it. To determine whether a potential goal (law) is consistent with your mission (constitution), ask the following question:

Will the pursuit of this goal direct me to become more like the person I have described in my mission statement?

Simply match up every potential goal to its corresponding role in your mission statement and confirm that the pursuit of that goal will cause you to grow into the type of person you ultimately want to be. If you can clearly and definitely answer "yes," then consider your goal to be constitutional.

Only when you know yourself can you know and deliberately fulfill your purpose in life. The following exercises will help you learn more about yourself and prepare you for writing a draft of your personal mission statement.

The Personal
Mission Statement Worksheet

1. What three qualities would you most like to see associated with your reputation?
A.
B.
C.

2. What three activities do you find most enjoyable?
A.
B.
C.

3. What three activities are most important to you?
A.
B.
C.

4. What three things would you like to change about your life if you had no restrictions or limitations?
A.
B.
C.

5. What six things do you want in life more than anything else? Be limitless in your thinking.
A.   D.
B.   E.
C.   F.

6. Who are the three people you admire most and why?
A.
B.
C.

The Personal
Mission Statement Worksheet

7. Of the people you admire most, what one quality do they all have in common?

8. What would you be willing to die for if you had to?

9. Why do you go to work in the morning?

10. What are your four most important roles in life (friend, salesperson, entrepreneur, student, uncle, husband, mother, etc.)?

A.   C.

B.   D.

11. What qualities would you like to be known for in each of these roles? (For examples see pages 32-33.)

A.   C.

B.   D.

12. What evidence would prove you have those qualities?

_____

_____

_____

The Personal
Mission Statement Worksheet

13. What three metaphors accurately describe your outlook? Why?

Life is a game.

Life is a bowl of cherries.

Life is the pits.

Life is a test.

Life is a competition.

Life is a gift.

Life is a dance.

Life is like a movie.

Life is a cycle of seasons.

Life is a struggle.

Life is like a school.

Life is a challenge.

Life is a sprint.

Life is a marathon.

Life is a gamble.

14. What would you like to see written on your tombstone?

15. If you could write your own eulogy, what would you want it to say?

The Personal
Mission Statement Outline

1. *25 word or less statement of purpose (one sentence)*
   My mission is to…

2. *Role A (Refer to Worksheet Questions 10-12)*
   a.. *Qualities/Description (1-2 sentences)*
   I am a…
   b. *Evidence, Actions, Responsibilities (1-2 sentences)*
   I…

3. *Role B*
   a. *Qualities/Description (1-2 sentences)*

   b. *Evidence, Actions, Responsibilities (1-2 sentences)*

4. *Role C*
   a. *Qualities/Description (1-2 sentences)*

   b. *Evidence, Actions, Responsibilities (1-2 sentences)*

5. *Role D*
   a. *Qualities/Description (1-2 sentences)*

   b. *Evidence, Actions, Responsibilities (1-2 sentences)*

6. *Summary and Conclusion (3-5 sentences)*
   Your personal philosophy of life and success

Lesson 2
Assignment

Using the outline provided on page 30, compose the first draft of your personal mission statement. Make sure it is written in present tense as if it were true today.

Ideal Qualities

accepting	dynamic	exceptional	confident
daring	intuitive	motivated	gentle
humble	quick	responsive	patient
precise	unique	charismatic	sincere
predictable	assertive	exemplary	understanding
achieving	efficient	neat	congenial
decisive	kind	responsible	genuine
humorous	rational	charming	passionate
predictable	smart	expressive	skillful
thoughtful	attentive	open-minded	conscientious
active	empathetic	reflective	goal-directed
dedicated	peaceful	cheerful	knowledgeable
imaginative	realistic	fair-minded	results-oriented
productive	considerate	optimistic	unpretentious
tolerant	attractive	sociable	good-natured
adept	encouraging	stimulating	perceptive
dependable	logical	clean	spiritually sound
independent	receptive	focused	consistent
professional	unstoppable	objective	graceful
trusting	authoritative	romantic	persistent
adventurous	energetic	strong	spontaneous

Ideal Qualities

determined	likable	coachable	cooperative
insightful	reassuring	forgiving	happy
proficient	vibrant	organized	personable
trustworthy	beautiful	self-aware	sexy
affectionate	enterprising	sympathetic	courageous
direct	loving	committed	helpful
intelligent	reliable	friendly	persuasive
prominent	vigorous	orderly	supportive
truthful	bold	self-confident	creative
agreeable	entertaining	talented	honest
disciplined	loyal	poised	compassionate
innovative	remarkable	fun	
prudent	warm	original	
unbeatable	brave	sensitive	
ambitious	enthusiastic	teachable	
distinctive	masterful	competent	
introspective	resourceful	fun-loving	
punctual	wise	outgoing	
unbreakable	caring	serious	
articulate	precise	steady	

Lesson 3

Choose to Write Down Compelling Goals

The very act of writing down and setting magnificent and compelling goals unlocks your creative powers, and the act of writing your goals is completely under your control.

Motivate yourself to stick with goal setting

Understand real goals are written goals

Learn a simple goal-setting process

Develop clarity about your future

Be able to share goals with someone you love

Manage your goals effectively

o you consider yourself an avid gambler? Most likely, you do not or you probably wouldn't be reading a book entitled *Success Is Not An Accident*. But if, at this moment, you don't have specific measurable goals written down for each area of your life, and a plan for their accomplishment, then the odds are that success for you will be an *accident*.

Like the toss of dice, if it happens at all, success for you will be random and haphazard. Cause and effect in your life will be unclear and confused. Your future will be unpredictable and your capacity to impact the world with your unique talents and gifts will be severely diminished. You will passively accept a life by default rather than assertively choosing a life by design. This approach is not for you.

Lesson 3 will stimulate and reinforce your need to set compelling goals, showing you how written goals and your mind are partners in your success. You will be motivated to do what is necessary to become the type of person you want to become. I'll explain why most of the country still doesn't set goals and show what you can do to avoid slipping into this dark trap of mediocrity. Understanding these concepts will prevent frustration and unnecessary trial and error. Next, I'll give you the eight rules or characteristics of effective goals and ways you can apply them to set yourself free from the limitations that hold back almost everyone. The foundation will be set and you'll be ready to begin your goal-setting workshop, where I'll guide you step-by-step through the actual goal-setting process. Once you learn and practice this process, you'll be able to adjust it, customize it and mold it so that you can apply it to achieve every goal you desire. Finally, I'll introduce you to a simple system for managing your long- and short-range goals.

Remember, goal setting is the master skill of all life-long success, yet it is practiced by less than 3 percent of the population. Even fewer, only about 1 percent, are fully goal directed. Someone who is goal-directed has committed to doing *only* those things that contribute to the accomplishment of a predetermined goal. Fortunately, goal setting and becoming goal-directed are skills just like typing, operating a computer, and selling. And like those skills, there is no limit to how good you can become if you are willing to practice and are committed to becoming an expert.

Unlike other skills, when you become goal directed, this expertise spills over into all other compartments of your life, drawing out your full potential in each area. As a seminar leader and personal coach, I'm sometimes questioned by my students and others who claim to be proficient in this vital area of life management already. They ask me to move on to more sophisticated principles and techniques. However, they soon realize that they have only an elementary understanding of the subject. Keep in mind that there is nothing more dangerous to your future success than assuming that you're good at a critical skill when your knowledge is rudimentary at best. Goal setting *is* a critical skill. Even those who are genuinely proficient at setting goals can dramatically increase their productivity by upgrading, refining and perfecting their goal achieving skills. To stay sharp at goal setting or any other skill, you must keep an open mind to new ways of doing things. You must not become satisfied or complacent. You must not think *good*. You must think *better*. If this sounds like your attitude and you are extremely serious about achieving greater personal and financial success, then the ideas in this lesson can help you progress further and faster than perhaps you ever thought possible.

You can be sure that investing the time and brain power to set meaningful goals in each area of your life will **produce internal, permanent motivation**. You'll become inner-directed, rather than outer- and other-directed. You'll experience an invigorating sense of control over your entire life. You'll be driven to become better and more competent with each passing day. Distractions and interruptions will no longer be a challenge for you because *your* course is set. Planning and reviewing your goals will provide you with an intense, laser-like focus. You will almost effortlessly concentrate on the vital few, instead of the trivial many. At every minute of every day you will know exactly where you need to be and what you need to be doing. This enhanced effectiveness *will* excite you and generate the enthusiasm and vitality necessary to become a peak performer.

You will notice yourself getting up earlier and staying up later, and you'll still have boundless energy. As you concentrate more and more on your goals, you'll think less and less about your problems and worries. Your energies will be directed toward worthwhile tasks, and you'll refuse to participate in senseless, "escapist," activities that only deplete your energy, distract you from your goals and delay your accomplishments. **Goals provide you with clarity of outcome,** which is the prerequisite for becoming an outstanding decision maker. When you know specifically where you're going, it's rather simple to assess opportunities and determine which ones are consistent with your objectives and which ones are not. Constantly remind yourself that every opportunity or activity is either moving you closer to the accomplishment of your goals, or it is moving you further away. The clock *is* always ticking. Nothing is neutral, and every single thing you do, or fail to do, counts!

While there are many important ingredients in the recipe of success, goals are most important. Without a doubt, the ability to set and achieve goals will do more to improve the quality of your life than any other single process you could ever learn. Whether we know it or not, we've all got goals. The challenge is that the majority of the population has such tiny goals that they have very little, if any,

Here's the Proof

At the beginning of an address to an audience of 150 employees at their annual company retreat, I asked everyone to stand up. Then I asked everyone who did not have goals to sit down. A handful of people sat. I then asked everyone who did not have **written** goals to sit down. Unfortunately, but not surprisingly, all but about 20 people sat. I then asked those remaining to sit down unless they had **written** goals for more than just their career or financial life. That eliminated another 12, leaving only eight of 150 people who had written goals in more than the financial area of their lives. I asked the remaining eight to sit down unless they had a written plan that accompanied their goals. That question filtered out five more, leaving three of 150 who had written goals and a plan in more than just the financial area. I asked the remaining three (all senior management, including the company president) to sit down unless they reviewed their goals on a daily basis. Only one person remained standing (a vice president of sales). Only one in 150 had written goals in more than the financial area, a plan for their accomplishment, and reviewed their goals daily. This is consistent with what I've found over the years as I've surveyed the attendees in my public events as well.

Invariably, less than 3 percent have written goals,

and even those who have written their goals down have often done so **only** in the financial or career area of their lives.

You may remember the study of 1953 Yale graduates. The subjects were interviewed and followed by researchers for more than twenty years. Then, the graduates were again interviewed, tested and surveyed. Results showed that 3 percent of the Yale graduates earned more money than all of the other 97 percent put together! The only difference was the top 3 percent had written goals and a plan of action for those goals, which they reviewed daily. Harvard University later studied business school graduates from the class of 1979. They found that, other than to "enjoy themselves," 87 percent of the class had no goals at all. Thirteen percent had goals and plans, but had not written them down. Only 3 percent of the Harvard class had **written** goals with a plan of action. In 1989, the class was resurveyed. The results showed that the 13 percent who had goals in their head were earning twice as much as the other 84 percent. But the 3 percent who had **written** their goals down and drafted a plan of action were earning ten times as much as the other 97 percent **combined**.

The point is clear: Having written goals will make you more successful and having written, well planned goals that you review daily will make you super successful.

motivational value. The masses tend to think small. It's as simple as that. And even those who have set high goals can get such a tremendous boost by **mastering the goal-setting principles**, that their lives will never again be the same. Most "could-be super achievers" *choose* to "wing it." And, they fail at life. They fail to develop the potential they were born with. Let's face it. We've all slacked off at some point. We've all settled for less than we could have had. So let's now, this minute, create a turning point! Let's together commit to raising our standards, to not slacking off. Remember *everything counts*!

Learning to set goals and crafting plans for their accomplishment will have more of a positive impact on your life than anything else you could possibly do. If you learn to set goals properly, you can learn anything else you want or need to learn. As the saying goes, "If you don't know where you are going, any road will take you there." Goals serve as points on a road map, detailing how to achieve success in a logical sequence. While this sounds so obvious, the unfortunate truth is that most people have taken it for granted. They have only a vague idea of where point A is, and no clue at all about point B. **Most people spend more time planning their summer vacations and their weddings than they do planning their lives and their marriages**. Most people **major** in **minor** things. They get caught up in the things that keep them busy but contribute very little to the overall quality of their lives. On the other hand, all great sports teams are known for mastering the fundamentals. They realize that if they simply practice the fundamentals over and over again, that everything else will take care of itself. What's that got to do with you? Well, just as athletes must master the basics of their particular sport, you too must master **the fundamentals of successful living** if you want to enjoy the rewards you were created to enjoy. Keep in mind that big goals generate lots of motivation and energy while small goals produce little, if any, motivation. The pursuit of your goals should be fun and interesting, like a cherished hobby. In other words, you need to design goals that really inspire you, that are

What is the most magnificent goal you can pursue in the next 3 years?

so interesting, motivating, and stimulating that you'll get up by 5 a.m. and stay up burning the midnight oil.

Intelligence, education, hard work, and good connections are useful, but without goals, you tend to drift like a rudderless ship from project to project, port to port, never really harnessing your full potential. Without goals, you can get by and even do well according to society's standards, but never come close to realizing your unique gifts. Without goals, you'll likely compare and measure yourself against others, rather than against your God-given potential.

Many have called goal setting the "master skill" of all lifelong success because it is the essential ingredient for successful living. Without it, you can never come close to being your best. With it, you can learn and master anything else you desire. But you can't become an expert at setting goals or master any other critical skill in life through just one exposure to a tape or by attending two or three seminars. Mastery doesn't come without deliberate, repetitive practice and a constant desire for never-ending advancement and improvement. There are many necessary fundamentals to successful living, but none of them will be of great value without mastering goal-setting skills. Do you know someone who is extremely well educated but has no goals? Of what practical use is an education if he or she can't apply the knowledge to some worthwhile purpose?

The primary benefit of mastering the skill of goal setting is that you begin to take **personal control of your**

life. The overwhelming majority of Americans are so caught up in the urgent activities of daily living that they seem to be sprinting in a dense fog. They are running hard but going nowhere. **They've confused activity with accomplishment.**

Without goals, one does not live; one simply exists, drifting in one direction, then another. Your life and your future will be determined by what comes along and attracts your attention. Denis Waitley wrote, "The reason most people never reach their goals is that they don't define them, learn about them or seriously consider them as believable or achievable. Winners can tell you where they are going, what they plan to do along the way, and who will be sharing the adventure with them." Those without clearly defined goals are tempted by every fad and every peer pressure society serves up. "Mediocrity" is best defined as failing to set big goals for your life. It will surprise you at how little in life you can become satisfied with if you don't set challenging goals routinely. It's really easy to gradually sink like a dense fog into accepting less than the best for yourself and for your family. Typically, someone who has slipped into this hole is the last to know. Unless you have goal-directed family and friends, it is likely nobody will ever tell you. Remember, the world is constantly recruiting more members into the mediocre 95 percent. This magnet of mediocrity is very similar to the concept of "misery loves company." **Mediocrity breeds mediocrity**. If a definite purpose is absent, you'll invariably drift in whichever direction the wind happens to be blowing. Instead of being assertive and proactive with your life, you'll simply react to the world around you and become, as most do, the self-induced victim of circumstances.

On the other hand, with a definite goal, you psychologically shield yourself from being influenced by current trends and distractions. You may see these fads and trends and even listen to some of them, but the existence of your

Top 10 Reasons to Establish Written Goals for Your Life

10. Written goals strengthen your character by promoting a long-term perspective.

9. Written goals allow you to lead your life as opposed to simply managing it.

8. Written goals provide internal, permanent, and consistent motivation.

7. Written goals help you stay focused — to concentrate on what's most important.

6. Written goals enhance your decision-making ability.

5. Written goals simultaneously require and build self-confidence.

4. Written goals help you create the future in advance.

3. Written goals help you control changes, to adjust your sails, to work with the wind, rather than against it .

2. Written goals heighten your awareness of opportunities that are consistent with your goals.

1. And finally, the Number One reason for writing your goals down, the most important benefit of setting effective goals, is the **person you become** as a result of the pursuit!

written definite goal will steer you quickly back to the pre-determined path.

People who experience long-term, consistent success avoid reaching into too many baskets. They deliberately concentrate on a single purpose that permits them to contribute the most and be their absolute best. With goals, you'll experience a daily sense of contentment because each day you will move closer and closer to the things most important to you! You'll be able to chart your progress and be inspired by what you've already done. As a result, you'll gain momentum and your successes will begin to snowball as your confidence grows and your ambitions expand. People without written goals don't have a sense of where they are in their lives. Like driving on an unmarked highway, they don't know if they're going north, south, east, or west. There are no mechanisms for constructive feedback and accountability. The positive pressure created by setting clearly defined goals activates your inborn creativity and allows your unique talents to rise to the surface. Without clearly defined goals and the corresponding pressure, it's impossible to develop into the high achiever you have the ability to become. You were created and blessed with unlimited potential and the ability to make your life a masterpiece. The least you can do is set challenging, specific goals that will force you to stretch and increase your contribution to others.

I hope I've sold you or resold you on the importance of goals and the impact they can have on you, your career, your family, and your future. I want you to not only know about goals, but to *live goals*! You can only function at your best as a human being and be your happiest, like a child on Christmas Eve, when you are actively pursuing a set of meaningful goals.

Psychological Blocks to Goal Setting

With all these benefits, why don't more people set goals? What are the psychological blocks that trick most people into just "winging it" through life? The next few pages will explain these "blocks," and show you *why* people fail so that you can be alert to these tendencies in yourself and in others.

> *Adapt an extended, long-term perspective. You excel in life to the extent that you apply a long-term perspective in making your most important decisions.*

I will explain the human characteristics that lead to under-achievement, frustration and mediocrity so you can recognize these behavior traits and consciously try to counteract and avoid them if they apply to your situation. If your objective is to develop and maximize your virtues, your successful qualities, it's very important that you also understand your vices, or the areas that may hold you back.

Why People Don't Set Goals

The number one reason why people don't set goals is that **they have not yet accepted personal responsibility for their lives**. Albert Schweitzer said, "Man must cease attributing his problems to his environment and learn again to exercise his will — his personal responsibility." The starting point of all greatness, of all personal success is the acceptance of 100 percent responsibility for your life. Until you have claimed total and unconditional responsibility for everything that happens in your life, you'll never be serious about goal setting. The irresponsible person is like a leaf blowing in the wind with zero hope of steering itself in a meaningful direction. "Whatever will be, will be! Qué sera, sera!" is the constant whine of the irresponsible person. He reasons that because *some* events are out of our control (such as stock market fluctuations, the weather, or the death of loved ones), *all* things must be out of our control. And so it goes. If things are out of our control, then why even bother trying to control them? After all, it's much more convenient and a whole lot easier to make excuses and put the blame for a mediocre life on someone else's shoulders. Remember this point as Emerson put it, "No one can cheat you out of ultimate success but yourself." Think about it. We may not like to hear this, but we've all been blessed with freedom of choice and we will go nowhere until and unless we accept complete and unqualified responsibility for our lives. Keep in mind that the prizes of life do not go to those who have been treated fairly, but to those who have maturely accepted responsibility.

The next reason why people don't set goals is the fear of criticism, often developed during childhood. Parents, teachers, and other adults often discourage us inadvertently by pointing out all the reasons why we can't achieve this goal or that goal. Their intentions are usually good. They don't want us to get our hopes up and then get disappointed. But the end result is that we stop creating compelling goals and dreams for ourselves and our futures because we don't want to experience the pain of having them squashed. Each time an authority figure reacts negatively to a child's expressed desire, the child becomes increasingly more hesitant to express those desires or goals. By the time we become adults the hesitancy to desire has become a reluctance to set goals, or at least goals that are out of the ordinary. **It is difficult to become goal-directed in a world that is centered on limitation**. Our peers often laugh at us when we talk about doing or becoming something they couldn't imagine for themselves. They may belittle or dampen your desire to start your own business or get into a career you truly love, or become a millionaire, or to really commit to growing in your faith. Since nobody

likes to be ridiculed, we learn
to shut up and keep our
dreams to ourselves,
eventually forgetting
what we wanted or
even why we embraced
those dreams. We learn
to play it safe, to go

Obstacles are the raw materials of great accomplishments.

along, not to rock the boat. Unfortunately, this attitude of conformity and underachievement is transported into adulthood where we continue to sell ourselves short, habitually and indefinitely.

The third reason why people do not set goals is that **they simply don't know how**. Even if you earn an advanced degree in our society, you've probably never had any formal instruction on how to set, manage, and achieve personal goals. Here is a serious void because goal setting is the master subject, the skill that makes all other subjects useful and practical. Herbert Spencer wrote, "The great aim of education is not knowledge, but action." At least it should be. Remember that to know but not to act is to not truly know. The only mistake worse than failing to master goal setting is assuming that you are competent at setting goals when your knowledge is limited at best. To think you know, but not really know, is a prescription for failure. I've spent countless hours studying the subject of goal setting and goal management. I've attended numerous live seminars on goal setting, read dozens of books and listened to hundreds of tapes on goals. I've taught many individuals and organizations how to effectively set goals. Even so, I personally learn something new or make a new distinction about goals nearly every day. That's why it amazes me to have others, who have read little or nothing about the process, tell me they already know how to set goals. Watch out for the unconscious incompetents, unaware of what they don't know.

7 Reasons People Don't Set Goals

1. They have not yet accepted personal responsibility for their lives.

2. They fear criticism.

3. They don't know how.

4. They don't realize the importance of goals.

5. The Curse of Early Success.

6. Fear of failure.

7. Fear of success.

The fourth reason people don't set goals is that **they don't realize the importance of goals**. If you grew up in a home where goal-setting and success were not topics of conversation, then simple ignorance can be holding you back. If your network of friends and acquaintances do not have clearly written goals, then it will be quite easy and natural for you to ignore your goals, and shrug them off as well. Be careful who you spend your time with, for you will inevitably start to think and act just like them.

The fifth reason why people don't set goals is what I call the **Curse of Early Success**. Many individuals experience success early in their lives, then become complacent and stop growing and improving. They may do well in college or they may get a prominent first job or maybe even a rapid promotion. Their early success, in effect, gives them a false sense of security. Those who fall prey to this curse are often pointed in the right direction but never do anything other than coast. This is a route of compromise. Who do you know who is making a "decent living" or earning "good money," but not doing a whole lot more with

> **When you choose to write down compelling goals, you are simultaneously choosing a compelling future. Exciting goals foreshadow an exciting future.**

their lives? When asked about their goals, these people give you a surprised stare and then reply that "they're on the right track." Settle, settle, settle is their theme song.

The sixth reason why people fail to set goals is the **fear of failure**. The fear of failure is, perhaps, the most common roadblock to goal-setting. Many people are afraid to set goals because they fear that by setting a goal they and others will be able to determine whether they have succeeded. This is an especially important point because those who fear failure are other- and outer-directed individuals. They're afraid of what others may think of them, and they are afraid of what they may think of themselves. People who suffer from the fear of failure harbor the subconscious thought, "If you don't try, you can't fail." Of course, this is nonsense — a convenient cop out. Winners know that the only true failure is the one who fails to try. **And failing to set written goals is the precise equivalent of not trying.** Winners also know that what applies to others does not necessarily apply to them, and so they follow their inner voice, rather than the outer voices of the masses.

Parents may promote the fear of failure in their children by making their love and praise conditional upon specific accomplishments. When a child believes that his parents' love depends on specific achievements, the child often becomes paralyzed with fear and unable to set challenging goals. The child finds more comfort in not trying than in risking failure. Conversely, the child who experiences *un*conditional love is likely to be assertive, ambitious, emotionally healthy, and eager to express himself or herself through a variety of pursuits.

Keep in mind that fear is a totally unnatural and unnecessary state of mind, regardless of the fact that it's very common. The Bible says, "God has not given us the spirit of fear, but of power, and of love, and of a sound mind." Psychologists say that newborns do have two fears, the fear of loud noises and the fear of falling. For the most part, though, we grow out of these fears, then later *learn* a series of other fears that are most often irrational. If nothing else, these fears are unproductive and inconsistent with the abundant and prosperous life we were created to enjoy.

And finally, the seventh reason why people don't set goals is the **fear of success**. The fear of success is a strange sounding concept, but nonetheless a predominant reason why many people fail to set goals. They are raised with the belief that it is somehow wrong or sinful to pursue our desires or to exceed the norms set by the masses. Therefore, many people "strive" to be just like everyone else, sometimes even apologizing for their accomplishments. In other words, they fear standing out or being different for any reason, even if it means sacrificing their success. Wouldn't it make more sense to emulate and conform to the peak performers rather than the underachievers. Don't we have enough of "the average" already?

A variation of the fear of success is the fear of failure at the next level. Some people are afraid that if they succeed it will put pressure on them to repeat their success. To avoid this pressure of having to "live up" to this new standard, they procrastinate and never give it their best, hoping that their lack of competence and confidence at the current level will remain a secret. This type of fear often manifests itself as subconscious, self-sabotaging behavior and is common both in the business world and in personal relationships.

Eight Rules for Highly Effective Goals

When you follow each of these eight rules you can expect to develop your full potential and join the top 1 percent of high achieving men and women. Many

Not knowing how you are going to accomplish a goal is never a valid excuse for not setting the goal. First, write the goal down. Then go to work to figure out how to reach it.

skeptics of goal setting and many underachievers have haphazardly attempted goal setting without following these rules, and failed as a result — erroneously concluding that goal-setting does not work, at least not for them. **Goals work for anyone who is subject to the law of gravity**. To ensure your success, follow these simple guidelines sincerely and the results will take care of themselves.

1. Highly effective goals are written!

This is by far the most important step in goal setting. Wishes and fantasies are transformed into goals through the act of writing them down. By writing your goals on paper, you make them concrete, tangible, and physically real. Remember all the studies that have shown that people who write their goals down are ten times more likely to achieve their goals than those who have their goals only "in their head." Similar research shows that people with written goals earn ten to 100 times more than equally gifted individuals who neglect to put their goals in writing. **Writing down your goals helps you to crystallize your thinking and gives you a physical device for focusing your**

attention. It stimulates your brain's reticular activating system, which is the mechanism within your brain that controls your awareness. When you are more conscious and aware of your goals, you will notice the people, resources, information and opportunities that will help you achieve your goals. Written goals also create a scorecard that you can evaluate and learn from. This scorecard acts as a measurement of your success and progress in life. Having your goals on paper increases your self-confidence. Being able to look down and see that you accomplished something you decided *in advance* to accomplish will give you a powerful sense of self-worth and will encourage you to set better and more challenging goals in the future. Your successes will begin to snowball! Writing goals on paper forms an accountability contract with yourself which automatically strengthens your character and boosts your self-confidence. Remember, in our society we assign a higher value to written agreements than oral agreements. They simply hold up better. So make your goals *written contracts with yourself!*

When people tell me they don't need to write their goals down because they "have it in their minds," I know they are really copping out and eventually will be missing out. You should state your goal as if its accomplishment were already a fact. For example, "I earn $125,000 this year," or, "I lower my handicap to 6 by June 1."

2. Highly effective goals are stated in present tense.

Writing goals like this allows you to recruit your mind to help you reach your goals. It creates what is called structural tension or dissonance in your mind when there is an obvious discrepancy between where you'd like to be and where you are currently. There's a gap between reality and your vision for the future and, since your mind hates tension of any kind, it immediately begins to alert you to all sorts of people, resources, and ideas that can help push you toward your goal. In essence, **it creates a new field of sight**. Stating a goal in the present tense communicates that goal to your brain in the most effective format, allowing you to clearly visualize your goal and start to really believe that it is possible for you. It signifies to your conscious and your subconscious mind that you are not where you want to be. Refuse to state your goal as, "I

> *If you don't have specific goals written down for your life, you are mentally malnourished. Your mind was designed to be fed with goals just as your body was designed to be fed with food and water.*

will do this," or, "I *will* accomplish that." When you use the term "I will," you mentally push your achievement somewhere off into the vague, distant future. There is less pressure to come up with the ideas and strategies to achieve your goal and less pressure for you to take immediate action. Using "I will" promotes procrastination and, of course, we want to put that off as long as possible.

3. Highly effective goals are stated positively.

For example, "I eat healthy, nutritious foods" instead of, "I no longer eat junk food." It's important to avoid stating, writing or talking about your goals in a negative way. You don't want to say, "I'm not going to hit the ball into the water." You should state it in positive terms because we think in pictures. Words are simply symbols for thoughts and ideas. Every time you write or say a word, you evoke a vision in your mind. And you can't evoke a vision of *not* doing something. You may say, "I don't eat junk food," but your *subconscious mind* only processes, "I eat junk food." It simply omits the "not" and shows you the "I eat junk food" vision. If you say, "I am not fat," it simply sees, understands, and goes to work on, "I am fat." If you say, "I am not hitting the ball into the water..." Again all your mind understands and goes to work on is "I am hitting the ball into the water." Now, you can play havoc with your golf friends by reminding them of the water right before they are about to take their shot. And they'll usually respond, "I'm not going to hit it into the water." But the reverse is often exactly what they do. **Remember, you'll always act consistently with the dominant pictures you allow to occupy your mind.** You must state your goal in a positive way so that your mind will understand it accurately and go to work on it. The reason most people state goals in negative terms is that they're much more aware of what they *don't* want. But whatever you're most aware of is what you experience. If you're aware of nice people, you'll start to bump into more nice people. If you're aware of your goals, you'll reach more of your goals. If you're aware of and conscious of prosperity and ways to serve others, you'll earn more money. And along the way, a lot of people will call you "lucky."

4. Highly effective goals are consistent with your personal mission statement.

Your goals should cause you to grow more like the person you were created to become. They should be goals that are personally meaningful to you. Many people make the mistake of setting goals that are meaningful to someone else or that will please someone else, but that have no passion in their own lives. The best way to keep a commitment to reach a goal is to understand why you are striving for it. It's the "why," or the link to your values, that keeps you motivated. Effective goals are best established *after* thoroughly thinking through your life and composing your personal mission statement. Values are those things that are most important to you in life. They include people, things, virtues, concepts, beliefs, and feelings. Together they constitute your individual philosophy of life or your personal vision. Goals are intended to satisfy or help you realize or experience your unique purpose in life. Trouble arises in our lives when we set goals without first clarifying what we stand for and who we want to become as human beings. We often accept and adopt the values of others because we've never invested the mental effort to determine what's truly important to us. When we set goals that are not in harmony with our personal values, we may still end up being high achievers, but the achievement will be accompanied by a feeling of emptiness, a feeling of "Is this it? Is this all there is?" Most unhappiness and negative stress in life comes from proclaiming internally that something or someone is most important to us, but then acting externally in a different way. Consider these questions:

> *It is when you establish and wholeheartedly pursue goals that are consistent with your highest values that you grow more like the person you were created to become, thereby satisfying and fulfilling your purpose.*

1. **Am I designing and organizing my life around principle-based values?**
2. **What am I becoming by pursuing this goal?**
3. **Will the accomplishment of this goal add to my peace of mind?**

Make sure that each of your goals is connected to a particular value or role in life. There should be a *deep* and *obvious* connection between your goals and your personal mission statement. The *pursuit* of your goals should force you to become more like the person described in your personal mission statement.

5. Highly effective goals are specific and measurable.

There must be no fuzziness or ambiguity whatsoever in the statement of your goal. A goal must be measurable so that you or someone else can objectively evaluate your progress and determine exactly when you have achieved the goal or if a new course of action should be taken. The more specific your goal is, the more clear you will be about what steps you must take to achieve it. Clarity attracts, so the more vivid you are, the more you will be focused on your goal. **The more you are focused on your goal, the more you'll be aware of the people, ideas, and resources around you that can help you reach that goal.** A clear and definite direction tends to increase your motivation and enthusiasm as well. It prods and spurs you to take action. Often in my coaching sessions clients ask, "How specific do I need to get on my goals?" I always answer, "Can you be more specific?" If it is possible to be more specific, then you should be. Just keep asking yourself: "How can I define this goal more clearly? How can I make it more precise?" You'll find that your creativity will increase as you more clearly define your goal. Creativity demands pressure. Being concrete and super-specific provides this pressure. Goals like, "I want to be happy," or, "I want to have a better marriage," or, "earn lots of money and be rich," don't cut it. They offer no clear, unambiguous goal to shoot for. Nothing is measurable. There is little or no purpose, and nothing much gets done. Vague and hazy objectives produce diluted results!

6. Highly effective goals are timebound.

Deadlines put positive pressure on you to take action. Otherwise it's just human nature to keep putting things off. Strangely enough, human beings tend to procrastinate on the goals that are the most valuable to their long-term peace of mind. We're funny in that we keep postponing those actions that can really increase the quality of our

Highly Effective Goals Are:

Written

Stated in the
Present Tense

Thoroughly
Planned

Stated
Positively

Timebound

Specific and
Measureable

Consistent with Your
Personal Mission
Statement

Challenging and
Reasonable

lives. We often get stuck in a rut, in the deadly confines of the comfort zone. **Comfort is often confused with success, and complacency is the result**. Make sure your goals are timebound with reasonable deadlines for accomplishment. It's very important that the time you allow is reasonable! It's been said that there is no such thing as an unrealistic goal, just an unrealistic time in which to accomplish it. Learn from each experience you have with goal setting so that you become progressively more accurate at setting deadlines.

7. Highly effective goals are reasonable and challenging.

They should cause you to stretch, to grow and get out of your comfort zone. In order to fully develop your potential, you *must* be willing to experience discomfort. It's often been suggested that you set goals with a 50-50 probability of success. You want to set goals that are achievable, but also build character by exercising your self-discipline and perseverance. In order for your subconscious mind to buy into your goal, it must have some degree of believability. For example, imagine you're driving a 15-year-old Chevy, but you've always had this thing for a Rolls-Royce. Think about pulling up at a traffic light in your Chevy and then a Rolls pulls up along side you. Would seeing that Rolls motivate you to take action — to drive straight to a Rolls-Royce dealer? Would it cause you to really want to stretch yourself? Would it be a powerful inspiration? Most likely it would not. The reason? The gap between where you are now — the old Chevy — and where you want to go — the Rolls-Royce — is simply beyond believability. Your mind would act as an enemy in that it just wouldn't accept the idea that you could be the owner of a Rolls Royce because there are no consistent prior experiences or beliefs. That doesn't mean there's no hope for you. **It just means that you need to set some intermediate** goals that act as step-ping stones to gradually raise your beliefs and self-concept to that of someone driving a **Rolls**. For instance, you could set a goal for driving a low-end luxury car

Your talent, skill, and creativity will rise to meet the level of goal you set for yourself. So think huge!

and another goal for driving the most expensive Mercedes. The point is to get your mind working with you, not against you. **And the way to accomplish this is to set goals that press the envelope, that are just slightly outside your current belief system.** Goals set in this manner activate your natural creativity, supplying you with ideas for achievement that otherwise would not have occurred to you. Goals that are unreasonable for you (at least at this point in your development) lock up your creativity and tend to act as de-motivators. As you become more of an expert at goal setting, as your confidence grows, you'll see how simple it is to incrementally strengthen your belief in your-self by setting and then achieving progressively more chal-lenging goals. You'll be able to set goals that may only have a 20 or 30 percent chance of success. But keep in mind that "reasonable" is different for everyone. Don't set them too low. If you're going to make a mistake, it is better to err on the side of setting your goals too high.

8. Highly effective goals are thoroughly planned.

You should have tangible action steps for each of your goals. You need to compile the details, make a plan, write out all the activities, prioritize them, time organize them, and rewrite them as often as necessary to make your plan perfect. Revise it, improve it, plan, and think on paper. It's also a good idea to consider developing several backup plans just as a good general would do. Exercise your mind by anticipating various contingencies and how you would respond in a swift and effective manner. All great leaders train themselves to be great planners.

The Goal Setting Workshop

Now, here is the most powerful, the most practical, and the most effective goal formula ever put together. If you will follow this method and exercise the self-discipline to put it into practice on a regular basis, your results will be out of all proportion to what you put into it.

Step #1: Brainstorm Your Dreams

Take out a pad of paper and a pen or pencil. Find a quiet place where you will not be disturbed for at least thirty minutes. At the top of a blank sheet of paper write the heading "The Next 30 Years." Now, begin to brainstorm about anything and everything you have ever wanted to be, do, or have. This is often called unlimited wishing or dreaming and it's the first tangible step in becoming goal directed. Creating this list requires no resources other than a small amount of time, some mental effort, and a few sheets of paper. And it will provide the foundation for a more successful, exciting, and fulfilling life. It will help you notice opportunities and possibilities because it stimulates your creativity. It's very important not to impose any limitations — real or imagined — such as money, age, sex, race, family, children, education, connections, or anything else. Watch out for letting limits turn into excuses that eventually spoil your opportunities for getting more out of life. Remember from Lesson 1, no matter how big your favorite excuse is or how perfect your alibi, somebody somewhere has had it far worse and still succeeded in spite of all perceived disadvantages. Limits only have power over you and your future to the degree that you let them.

Suspend *all* judgment on whether or not you can achieve what you want or whether you are worthy of it. **Just write it down**!

There is no limit, other than the power of your imagination, to the number of desires or wishes you can include on your own personal wish list. The key to this exercise is to write down everything and anything you can imagine without letting your mind stop. Think of your wish list as a grand script for the movie of your life! You are, after all, the writer, producer, director, and star of your own life. You can take your movie in any direction you choose and you can fill the script with as much passion, adventure, joy, and positive experiences as you can imagine or desire. Remember that what you write down is your preview of life's coming attractions. For additional ideas and a list of legendary achiever John Goddard's lifetime goals, please see the appendix, pages 200-208.

You will find that just completing this simple brainstorming process will produce a renewed sense of enthusiasm for your future. There will be an inner excitement, a surge of vitality and positive anticipation. You'll want to revise and review this list at least once a year. Many of my clients have found this exercise so refreshing and stimulating that they practice it two or three times a year. Try it for yourself and see.

Now that you've written down everything you could ever possibly want, look over your list and make sure you have some challenging financial goals. Make sure you have some goals for your marriage or for your primary relationship. Do you have fitness goals? Are there any new health habits you could develop? What about your personal growth? What new things do you want to learn? How many books do you want to read next year? Did you write down any spiritual goals? This time next year, do you want to be in the same place spiritually?

If you want to make it happen, you'd better write it down.

Questions to help you start your brainstorm session

Remember, no limits!

- What do you want to have?
- What do you want to be?
- What extraordinary things would you like to do?
- What kind of impact do you want to have on your profession?
- How could you turn one of your hobbies into a business?
- Where do you want to go? And who do you want to go with?
- What would you like the quality of your marriage to be?
- What do you want to share?
- What charities do you want to support?
- How much money do you want to donate in your lifetime?
- Would you like to get a massage every week? How about every day?
- Would you like to skydive or scuba dive?
- Would you like to have a personal trainer? How about a personal success coach?
- Are there any famous people you would like to meet? Would you like to become famous? And by excelling at what?
- How much passion do you want to have in your marriage?
- Would you like to become a millionaire? How about a billionaire?
- Do you want to work for someone else the rest of your life?

More Brainstorming Questions

- *What would you like your net worth to be when you retire? At what age would you like to retire?*

- *What new things would you like to learn?*

- *Would you like to conquer the fear of public speaking?*

- *What character traits would you like to develop?*

- *What silly things would you like to do?*

- *If you had unlimited time, talent, finances, knowledge, self-confidence, and support from your family, how would your life change?*

- *What one great thing would you dare to attempt if you knew, if you absolutely knew, you could not fail?*

Think about the many areas of your life: family and home, spiritual, health and fitness, relationships, social, career/financial, your personal development. Make sure you have goals for each area. To lead a happy, balanced life, you need a balance of goals. So, whatever it is, write it down. **Write it down!**

Step #2: Create Your Ideal Lifestyle

Proper planning requires that you look into the distant future and create a vivid mental image of the life you'd like to be leading. This will become your personal vision for the future. The number of years you project into the future can vary depending upon your experience with goals and your current level of comfort. Some of my clients go as far out as 30 years; others use 9 to 21. The point is to develop as much clarity as possible about the vital details of the life and lifestyle you'd like to be enjoying in the future. The reason for going so far into the future is that, eventually, you're going to end up there. In order to make sure your actions and choices of today match up with the life you want tomorrow, you must begin with the end result in mind. You have to know where you're headed. **You cannot effectively lead your life if you only have short-term goals.** It takes a long-term vision and long-range goals to reveal the most appropriate short-term goals. So mentally project yourself into the future. Try for at least 9 years.

Using the ideas generated from your brainstorm in step one, write a two or three paragraph description of your ideal lifestyle. Write in the present tense as if it were already true. Look at your life as an integrated whole. Approach life with the big picture in mind.

Be sure to include details about your health, marriage, faith, major accomplishments, things you're grateful for, hobbies, energy level, net worth, amount of free time, peace of mind, and anything else you can think of. Make it a priority to become the most well-rounded, effective human being you can become. Now, make a note of the most obvious milestones or signposts you would have to see along the way in order to experience the life you have just described. You can view these benchmarks as the sub-goals that need to be met before your long-term vision can become a reality.

Step #3: Take the 3-Year Leap

Now that you have some ideas about your future, let's tackle the mid-term by creating clear, specific, measurable, achievable, and most importantly *written* 3-year goals and their corresponding plans for accomplishment. I've found that three years is the perfect amount of time to manage and do really big things with your life. It's the ideal length of time to visualize your life being significantly different. **Three years is long enough to achieve some gigantic goals but not so far out that it loses its motivational pull.** Your 3-year goals, from today to 3 years out, are intended to be sub-goals or milestones on the way to your

The Goal Achievement Formula

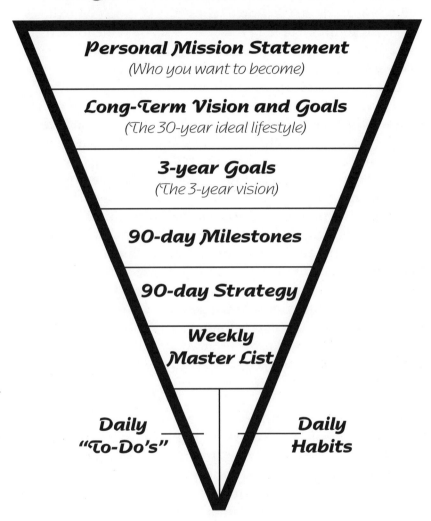

Personal Mission Statement
(Who you want to become)

Long-Term Vision and Goals
(The 30-year ideal lifestyle)

3-year Goals
(The 3-year vision)

90-day Milestones

90-day Strategy

Weekly Master List

Daily "To-Do's"   **Daily Habits**

long-term vision. So make sure that they are in alignment by asking the question, "Will the accomplishment of these goals lead me to my vision?" How so exactly? Double check yourself by asking, "Does the pursuit of my 3-year goals represent the best path or route to my long-term vision?" After all, it's your vision of the future that should determine your 3-year goals.

Once you've established that your 3-year goals *will* carry you to your vision, it's time to convince yourself why these goals are so important.

Step #4: Convince Yourself

Next, list all of the rewards. What's in it for you? Why do you want to achieve this goal? Keep in mind that motivation is directly proportionate to the number and intensity of reasons you want to do anything. There will be tangible rewards and intangible benefits. Think about the feelings and emotions you'll enjoy as a result of achieving your goal and think about the material or tangible rewards you'll receive. Write them down. Exaggerate a little bit. The more powerful you can make this purpose, your "why," the better. Make sure you have enough reasons for accomplishing your goals. If you have enough reasons, you can accomplish anything. Keep in mind that reasons precede answers. Reasons come first. Then the answers or action plan. Determine the *what*. Figure out the *why*, and then the *how*! When you know what you want and when you want it badly enough, you can always find a way to make it happen.

Step #5: Plan on Paper

Planning is the hallmark of the mature, responsible, and self-reliant human being. In fact, almost every failure can be traced back to lack of proper planning.

Planning is the deliberate act of pulling the future into the present, so you can do something about the future right now. **You must change your habits and other behaviors now to reap rewards in the future.** If you want your future to be different, you must make things different in the present. **Things don't improve by themselves!** You must do different things to bring about the new results you're seeking.

Many people don't understand what planning is. They

> **All great leaders possess tremendous long-term clarity about what they're trying to accomplish both in their careers and personally. And it's this long-term perspective that builds character, wisdom, and self-discipline. Long-term thinking is the hallmark of high performance living, yet it's often neglected in favor of the treadmill of hectic, urgent "activities of the moment."**

interpret the word "planning" as simply the transferring into their calendar of miscellaneous appointments and to do's as they happen to pop up from the backside of envelopes, cocktail napkins, and miscellaneous Post-it notes without any regard to long-term goals or a personal mission.

Planning really means evaluating your life in light of where you've been, where you are now, and where you intend to go. **You must be willing to question how well you've managed your life up until now.** Effective planning allows you to avoid life management by crisis. Crises divert your attention from the vital people and activities in your life and are nearly always a result of inadequate planning. Systematic, long-term, yearly, quarterly, monthly, weekly, and daily planning is absolutely critical to your success. Remind yourself that all successful people plan on paper. Unsuccessful people simply "can't seem to find the time."

Be aware, however, that plans are hardly ever 100 percent accurate. But you must not fall in the trap of thinking, "Well, since I cannot have a perfect plan...since I cannot eliminate all interruptions...since I cannot eliminate all urgencies...therefore, why even bother to eliminate any of them?" That's crooked logic and a cop-out for failing to try. Let go of any tendencies you have toward misplaced perfectionism and focus instead on the strategic planning that will take your life to a higher level. Invest considerable time on your plan. Keep in mind that you will be rewriting, revising, and improving your plan as you progress toward your goals.

The starting point of 3-year planning is to see yourself already in possession of your 3-year goals, then work back to the present. This means that you must mentally project yourself into the future to the time and place where your goal will be a reality. From this vantage point look back to the present and critically assess the steps you must take to reach your goal. This "back from the future" exercise will sharpen your perception and solidify your strategy. It develops the habit of outcome-based thinking or results orientation.

This is helpful for your short-term goals as well as major lifetime goals. Constantly feed your mind a clear, vivid picture of the ideal end result you're striving for. Then, develop your plan by working from the accomplishment of the goal back to the present.

In other words, your 3-year goals should be, in essence, action steps or sub-goals leading up to your long-term vision.

It's easy to talk about what we want, but the hard part is putting plans on paper, where it actually means something.

So, from the perspective of having accomplished your 3-year goals, begin to work your way back to today. Consider what must be accomplished by the end of year two and then by the end of year one. At this point, the end of year one, you have a set of one-year goals. To translate all this into action, think about what you need to accomplish

> **Envision yourself having accomplished your goals. Stand on the mountaintop and look down at where you have been. See what you have achieved to reach your goal. What was the last step you took? Write that down. The next-to-last step? Write that, too. Retrace your steps back down the mountain, writing all the way. The words you write will become your landmarks as you climb the mountain in reality and achieve your goals.**

in the 4th quarter. What do you need to accomplish by the 3rd quarter? The 2nd quarter? And, finally, in quarter number 1? This is the basic concept of strategic planning. As you can see, we're counting backwards in time from a mid-range goal to an immediate plan of action. We've gone from 3 years down the road and backtracked to the end of the current year and so on to the 3rd, 2nd, and 1st quarters — creating a chronological list of stepping stones that will ultimately result in the accomplishment of your 3-year goals.

Step #6: List Available Resources

Now, write down all the resources available to you to help you reach your 3-year goals. Who or what could help you reach your goals? What books, tapes, mentors, coaches, seminars, information, technology or other resources could you use in the accomplishment of your goal? Identify the organizations and groups with which you'll need to create alliances.

Step #7: List Potential Obstacles

Now that you've written down all the potential resources, take a moment to think about what could *prevent* you from reaching your goals. Do you have any habits, attitudes or beliefs that may hinder your progress? How will you personally need to change and grow before this goal can be reached? What about your finances? What about undeveloped skills? Have you mastered the vital skill of time management? What else could keep you from reaching this goal? List all the possible obstacles you may encounter. Think of this as contingency preparation or crisis anticipation planning. Better safe than sorry. Include anything that may hinder you in reaching your goal. It may seem a little negative to mention these obstacles, but obstacles aren't necessarily negative. It depends on how you interpret them and what you do with them. If you write down the obstacles and take a good look at each one, you often find that the obstacles don't even exist. **Obstacles that loom huge in your mind tend to shrink when they're written on paper.** Any major or worthwhile goal has obstacles. Obstacles build your goal-achieving muscles. They hold the raw materials of exciting opportunities. And if there are no obstacles, it's not even really a goal. It's simply busywork. Activity. And if it's just busywork, don't expect it to shower you with lots of exciting rewards upon completion.

> *Remember, your 90-day milestones lead to the accomplishment of your 3-year goals.*

Step #8: Identify Ways to Overcome Obstacles

Next, list some ideas to overcome the obstacles you just wrote down. List all the solutions to possible obstacles. Approach each one with the feeling that you already have a good solution. Look at each obstacle as a challenge or a problem waiting to be solved. **We often don't realize it, but we frequently come face-to-face with the exact obstacle we need at just the right time to sharpen us where we need it the most**. All challenges, if dealt with directly and swiftly, will make you stronger, better, and wiser. Challenges or setbacks are intended to teach us something. They prepare us for performing more effectively at the next level. Just as it's necessary to bench press 150 pounds before you try 200 pounds, and to get a little bit sore, it's also necessary to overcome obstacles along the path to our goals. **And the more ambitious you are, the more challenges will be thrown your way.** Again, many times, if not always, great opportunities arise when you encounter obstacles, and these opportunities become more apparent when you maintain a positive, resourceful attitude and when you take time to analyze the situation or obstacle in a relaxed state of mind. To paraphrase Booker T. Washington, success is not measured so much by our accomplishments in life, but by what we had to overcome in the process. Keep in mind that we're goal-striving organisms. We're engineered to solve problems and we function best and are happiest when we're moving toward a goal.

Following Through After the Workshop

Now, to actually implement and coordinate a concrete system for keeping up with your list of goal-directed activities, use three lists. First, a quarterly strategy list of everything you must do to accomplish each of your 90-day milestones. From that, select the most important items to create your weekly objectives or Weekly Master List. Then, plan each day from that. So, you've gone from a long Quarterly strategy List to a Weekly Master List down to a few manageable items for each day — all leading you toward your 3-year vision.

Lesson 3
<u>*Assignments*</u>

1. Write down 150 goals for the next 30 years of your life. (See appendix, pages 200-208 for thought stimulators.

2. Choose 5 goals to focus on for the next 3 years. Make sure you have a well-balanced set of goals.

3. Using the "Back from the Future" technique, plan the accomplishments of your goals on paper.

4. Begin the power habit of rewriting your top 5 goals each morning.

<u>*Lesson 4*</u>
Choose to Invest Your Time Wisely

You can't make more time —
only better choices.

Minimize wasted time

Work smarter

Reduce stress

Stay organized

Experience inner peace

Learn 21 time savers

*T*he pages that follow provide powerful, usable and highly effective time management strategies that have made a dramatic impact on the lives of my clients as well as countless other successful individuals.

Before we begin, let me make a point about human nature. In addition to being quite amusing, human nature is also the great arch rival of personal effectiveness. I routinely conduct time management workshops and seminars for both large and small organizations in a wide variety of industries. Inevitably though, no matter who my audience happens to be, I hear the identical cries:

"But our situation is unique"
or
"Our business is such that it's impossible to properly plan, delegate, organize, hold effective meetings, or otherwise practice solid, proven time management habits"
or
"That won't work for us because of this, that, or the other."

Nonsense! Let me translate what these naysayers really mean. These people are really saying: "Due to the nature of our particular business, we're forced to operate inefficiently." Think about that for a second. "Due to the nature of our particular business, we're forced to operate inefficiently." Doesn't that sound a bit crazy?

The common thread to these comments is none other than human nature. All human beings have a natural inclination to resist change,

Rapid-Fire Time Saver #1

Communicate to every employee what five minutes of wasted time means on a company-wide yearly scale. Relate those numbers to profits and salaries.

and nothing is quite as challenging as changing a bad or self-defeating habit. We tend to want our lives and businesses to improve, but sometimes not quite so badly that *we are willing to change*. But remember this, if any area of your life is to get better, you must get better. This means *you* must be willing to replace bad, sloppy habits with the habits of success and peak performance. Aristotle reminded us thousands of years ago, "We are what we repeatedly do." And if you're committed to repeatedly applying the principles in this lesson, you will not believe the difference!

Make sure you don't fall into the trap of thinking that your time constraints are unique and unmanageable. It doesn't matter where or how you're currently living. You can live in the projects or in a mansion on the hill or anywhere in between, but one thing remains constant...**No matter who you are, your progress and success in life will depend more than any other factor on how you invest the 24 hours you're blessed with each day.** In fact, contrary to popular belief, or the "politically correct" view, it's not just the most talented, gifted, well-educated, affluent, or advantaged people who achieve outstanding results in life. Nor is it the most intelligent, the hardest working, or the most creative. As I emphasized in Lesson 1, success in life comes from one thing: from *deciding* exactly what it is you want to accomplish and then deliberately *choosing to invest* the minutes and hours of your life doing only those things that move you in the direction of your goals. This lesson will give you the "street smarts" to do just that.

If you're willing to seize the initiative, you can learn time management just like you can learn to use a computer, play a sport, or any other skill you desire to master. The more ambitious you are, the

Rapid-Fire Time Saver #2

Consider a convenient hideaway to isolate yourself. It can be in the same building, at home or close to your home or even in your car parked in a quiet space.

better you must be at squeezing every last bit of usefulness out of every minute at your disposal, because if you don't make the most out of an hour or even a minute, you'll never get a second chance with it. Misusing just 15 minutes a day over a year can cost you 90 hours, or more than two full work weeks. Remember, whether you want to admit it or not, many people are even busier than you, but they accomplish more hour to hour, day to day. They obviously don't have more time. They just put their time to greater advantage. And you can do that as well!

What is *Time*?

Time is a unique and interesting resource, invisible, unalterable, and unstoppable. Everyone has the same amount of time. You and I must live on 86,400 seconds, 1,440 minutes, 24 hours each day, 168 hours a week, approximately 720 hours per month, 8,640 hours per year, 177,800 hours over the next 20 years and about 691,200 hours if we live to be 80 years old. And each segment of time you receive must be instantly spent.

> ## *Vital Time is the quantity of time you invest in principle-based, goal-directed activities.*

If you want to minimize wasted time, work smarter, maximize your productive capabilities, and experience more Vital Time, then this lesson is for you. If you want to work less, but earn even more, then this lesson is for you. These pages contain the essence of the most practical and usable ideas and techniques ever developed on the subject of time effectiveness. Each strategy and tactic presented has been field-tested and proven to be workable in the challenging arena of modern living.

In fact, I put many of the techniques you're about to learn into practice specifically in order to complete this book. After completing this project, which required countless hours of research, writing, editing, and even more editing (which had to be done around my previous commitments and already full schedule), I'm more convinced than ever of the validity and usability of the ideas I'm about to share with you. The book you have in your hands is evidence of my personal triumph over procrastination and the other real and imagined diversions that hold most people back. By consistently and diligently applying these principles, you'll have more time for yourself, your family and your friends.

You can approach the following ideas like you would an enormous dinner buffet. Just as you would not, or at least should not, eat everything on the buffet, it's not necessary or even recommended that you try to apply every single tactic we discuss in order to satisfy your time management appetite. I'd like for you, more than anything else, to concentrate on the most nutritious and most overlooked portion of time management, which is what I call Vital Time.

Rapid-Fire Time Saver #3

During breaks in the workday, or when coming and going, use the stairs. It's a great way to maximize the use of that time and to burn up extra calories.

These are the activities that are often squeezed out of your schedule by the addictive urgencies of daily living. It's been said that all behavior or action of any sort is an expression of your character. If you put these recommendations into practice, it will allow you to engage in Vital Time, that time which allows you to express who you are and what you believe in. Remember, the intent

I Didn't Have Time

It has been said that four simple words characterize mediocrity most accurately and they are, "I didn't have time." Four simple words. "I didn't have time." There is no excuse more damaging that you or anyone else could have concerning success. When you tell someone else that you didn't have time, you simply reinforce their perception of you as someone who can't be relied upon to get the job done. And when you tell yourself that you didn't have enough time, you undermine your inner credibility and fortify a self-image of underachievement and irresponsibility.

of time management is to **enhance the quality and balance** of your life, not simply to speed it up!

Your Self-Image Affects The Way You Manage Time

Creating Vital Time requires that you understand how the internal picture you hold of yourself affects your ability to make the best use of your life. Your self-image affects how well you spend your time because when you have a positive self-image with regard to time management, you feel in control rather than as though you're simply reacting to external pressures. You have the ability to take the events of your life and organize them so they make sense. The first step to becoming someone in control, someone who is an outstanding manager of his time, is to explore and improve your self-image.

Formed primarily from your suggestive environment, your self-image is the subconscious mechanism responsible for guiding your behavior. The importance of this is that **we always act consistently with the image we have of ourselves.** So if you see yourself as someone who is overly busy with far too many things to do, someone who is disorganized or working too hard, then your attempt at mastering your time will be in vain. Your weak self-image serves as a veritable handcuff to your abilities and hampers your efforts at controlling your time. In fact, you cannot expect to behave in a way different from your self-image programming any more than you could expect to put a chocolate cake mix in the oven and an hour later take out an apple pie. You always get out only what you put in.

Your self-image regulates your behavior just like a thermostat

Rapid-Fire Time Saver #4

Measure your time in small increments, like .6 of an hour. Attorneys do it. It creates awareness, speed, and momentum.

controls the room temperature. It determines how you use your time, knowledge, skills and experiences. And remember, we don't question the validity of our self-image. We simply proceed to behave as if it were true.

So the key to becoming an outstanding time manager is to start thinking of yourself and speaking of yourself as an outstanding time manager. If someone asks you about your day, tell them, "Today is the best day I've ever had. I've managed my time perfectly today. I don't have time to tell you anymore now because I've got things to do." Vocalize, verbalize and then actualize.

Changing your language or terminology changes your self-image. Changing your self-image changes your attitude. And changing your attitude changes your actions. I often like to say, "Attitude outranks facts." Think, "How would I act if I were already an excellent time manager? How would I act if I were the most effective time manager in the world?"

Imagine someone offered you $20,000 to play the part of an excellent time manager in a movie. What are some of the things you would do? Well, you would sit up straight, you'd have your desk organized. You'd move quickly. You'd work on one thing at a time. You'd work from a list. You'd anticipate and plan for interruptions. Shakespeare said, "Act the part, become the part." If you start acting like an excellent time manager, really pretending you're *already* a model of personal effectiveness, the habits will lock in like a vise, and soon you will become an excellent time manager in reality.

Rapid-Fire Time Saver #5

Prepare a complete set of all your important keys and then make as many duplicate sets as necessary. Then, no matter which set you pick up, you will never be locked out of your home, office or the car you choose to drive. If you have a separate set of keys for each set of locks, you're likely to end up at the right lock with the wrong keys! And, always leave your keys in the same spot.

Vital Time Tactic #1:
Overcome Procrastination

You must win the battle against procrastination to rise above the average and create Vital Time. If that were not one of your objectives, you probably would not be reading this book. Peak performance and procrastination are simply incompatible. It's been said that tomorrow can only be found in the calendar of fools. This is completely accurate.

Procrastination, which is the delaying of higher priority tasks in favor of lower priority ones, is more responsible for frustration, stress, and under-achievement than any other single factor. It is the art of keeping up with yesterday and avoiding today. Procrastination causes emotional anguish, devastates personal relationships, wrecks any attempt at effectiveness, and promotes physical and mental exhaustion. Procrastination is all about excuses, and you know as well as I do that the excuses you have today are the excuses you will have tomorrow. Today's excuses are but the ancestors to tomorrow's excuses and the predecessors to future mediocrity.

So how can you defeat procrastination and start creating Vital Time? Most often the hardest part of getting started is getting started. Once you're involved, you've overcome the highest hurdle. And you don't always have to start at the beginning. If the first step seems hard or too large, start with another part of the project. Or, set a mini-goal, such as working at something for 15 minutes, whether it's reading, exercising or a work project. Often, after 15 minutes, you'll want to continue. You may even complete the entire task. I used a kitchen timer set on 15 minutes to get me in the habit of daily reading. I usually ended up reading much more, and

Rapid-Fire Time Saver #6

Develop binders of commonly sought materials. You'll avoid sorting through files to retrieve the answers to frequently asked questions.

7 Ways to Procrastinate Effectively
(A parody)

1. *Just wish and hope and dream. There's really no need to ever set clear, specific goals and then roll up your sleeves and get to work.*

2. *Always work on what's fun and easy, C & B tasks, rather than doing A priorities, the things that are often hard, but necessary. Don't low-priority tasks build momentum?*

3. *Stay in your career even if you find yourself unhappy, stuck, and unable to grow. You can always look forward to the evenings and weekends.*

4. *Always delay difficult work if you're sleepy or tired! Use fatigue strategically to escape those uncomfortable tasks.*

5. *If you fear something is wrong with you physically, don't see a doctor. That way you can avoid dealing with the reality of a possible illness. It's much easier to wait until you're really sick.*

6. *Tomorrow is always a good day to start something important, such as exercising or a diet. Next week is even better.*

7. *Take a break from all projects when you hit the 90 percent completion mark. That way you'll always have them to come back to.*

that habit is now ingrained as a part of my daily routine. Break large jobs down into small pieces or daily do-ables. As the saying goes, "You can only eat an elephant piece by piece."

Develop a sense of urgency, a "do it now" attitude, a bias for action. And use a fast tempo. The faster you are, the more productive you'll be. You'll get less fatigued, believe it or not, walking fast, doing things fast, getting out and moving than you will if you're trudging around.

Learn to make decisions fast as well. Successful people take little time to make a decision and a long time to change a decision once it has been made. Good decision making involves knowing and anticipating what the options are and assessing how important the pluses and minuses may be. Develop a system that you use consistently when making decisions. Get input from good decision-makers and learn from them. And remember, it's better to make a bad decision that directs your course than to make no decision at all. Making no decision produces stagnation and triggers feelings of failure and confusion and worry. It's been said even the best of plans die flat if you're consumed by indecision and make no move to put the plan into action. Be a doer, not a wisher or a hoper.

If your life is to get better, you have to do something constructive to make it better, and there's nothing more constructive than eliminating procrastination from your life.

Rapid-Fire Time Saver #7

Schedule your most difficult tasks during your most productive time of the day.

Vital Time Tactic #2
Organize Your Workspace

You must have a strategically organized work space. You can practice all the other time management principles, but if you remain disorganized you're going to severely restrict the effectiveness of the other

7 Valid Reasons to Procrastinate

(A parody)

1. Most obviously, putting things off allows you to escape from unpleasant activities. These could be things that you're afraid to do or simply things that you don't enjoy doing.

2. If you <u>wait</u> for things to get better, you can still blame the world for your unhappiness. Enough of that personal responsibility stuff.

3. You can subtly manipulate others to do the job. If you put it off long enough, somebody else may eventually have to step in and do it for you.

4. You can avoid the continuing and increased responsibility that goes with success. If you do a job well and on time, others will only expect you to do it again. This, of course, is grossly unfair.

5. If you don't feel like doing the job now, plan to do it later. Some call this laziness, but they're rude.

6. You can claim perfectionist immunity. Because you're so conscientious, others will understand if you never get started.

7. If you're not sure, wait. This is a good rule of thumb. A difficult, overwhelming or insurmountable task should always be delayed until you're absolutely ready and well rested.

principles you practice. **Most disorganization tends to come from indecision, not being able to decide if a piece of paper or some other information is important or not and if it is, what to do with it.** This is manifested in the habit of picking up the same things three or four times, having a constantly overstuffed "in" box and having multiple stacks of papers, periodicals and files lying around the office. If your office is typical, roughly three quarters of the items in your files should have been placed in the trash.

On and around your work space, divide all objects into one of two categories: Tools and Supplies. Tools are reusable items like the stapler, telephone, tape holder, scissors and letter openers. Supplies are consumable items like staples, tape, Liquid Paper, paper clips, Post-It notes, and letterhead. Keep tools and supplies in a separate storage area, such as a drawer, on a shelf, or in cabinets.

Use an in/out box. Check the box at least twice daily at specific, pre-determined times. Appropriately file or act upon all incoming materials immediately. To maximize your effectiveness and productivity, avoid handling any item more than once. Also, it's a good idea to stand up as you sort your in/out box and you'll move faster and save even more time.

Rapid-Fire Time Saver #8

If you make an appointment well in advance, call the day before and remind the other person of it. This is professional and it saves time and embarrassment.

Every time something comes to your desk, ask, "Is it an action?" In other words, is it a "to do"? Is there some specific action I must take on it or is it a support, a reference, or some sort of information that I may need to access sometime later? If it's something you may need to access later, put it in the appropriate file category and then alphabetize the information in that file. If it's an action or "to do," place it one of three action categories:

• The routine "to do" files if it's a recurring, routine task such as "to read," "write letters," or "call back."

> *Successful people have successful habits. Mediocre people have mediocre habits. And it all starts with a choice.*

• The priority "to do" files if it's a task that must be done in order of importance.

• The tickler "to do" files if the task needs to be completed on a specific future date.

Categorize everything. Use hanging files and, if possible, don't waste time by placing manila file folders inside hanging file folders. In most instances, no manila folders are necessary at all. Color code your hanging files by category using colored files, tabs, or both. Category should be indicated by a colored tab at the far left followed by staggered, coordinating tabs for the related subjects and topics in each category. For example, "marketing" might be the category, "direct mail" might be the subject, "catalog" might be the topic and the number, title, or item might be the "Spring 1995 issue" of the catalog.

Type out your system for easy reference in the event your assistant, another co-worker, or family member must access the files. For example, purple might be action files; green, client files; blue, research and reference; yellow, administrative; and red, marketing. Then create an index or table of contents listing the files in each category. Update this index regularly to prevent losing

Rapid-Fire Time Saver #9

Respond to mail by telephone or e-mail when you can. If possible, delegate the response.

files in your system. **This takes a little bit of your time up front but saves time in the long run.**

Next, a messy, disorganized desk can and will weigh you down. In fact, according to the Principle of Correspondence, your outer life is a mirror image reflection of your inner life. Everything you say and do, including how organized you are, is a reflection of the real you! If you constantly have a cluttered work area, it's a sign that you've got stress and turmoil going on inside that needs to be dealt with. The simple act of cleaning up your work area can make you feel more in control of your life and can help you be more effective, more efficient, and more optimistic.

Most importantly, the cleaner your work area, the fewer things that are on your desk, the more you will get done. As you go up higher and higher in organizations the desks get cleaner and cleaner. And that's no coincidence.

Vital Time Tactic #3
Handle reading material more efficiently

To be effective in today's rapidly changing society, it's crucial to stay current with what's going on. So here are three keys to handling reading material.

First, become a speed reader. A course in speed reading will enable you to double or triple your reading speed almost instantly. I more than doubled my speed in the first two hours. Courses are available in live seminars as well as on audio-cassette. Courses in "photo reading" or accelerated learning are new approaches you may want to investigate as well. The remarkable results you get from practicing these simple methods will definitely surprise you.

Another way to accelerate your

Rapid-Fire Time Saver #10

Develop a master-mind group of success-minded people who can accelerate your progress toward your goals.

reading is to go straight to the table of contents, flip through the book quickly, get to the chapter that is most important to you, then read that chapter or mark it for future reference. Often, you'll find out the material is not even worth reading at all, which, of course, speeds up your reading considerably.

Read only top priority articles in magazines, publications, journals, newsletters, and so on. Again, read the table of contents, pick the items that are of the most interest to you, go right to those items, tear out the pages, put the pages in your "to read" file, and always take it with you to read during what I call "transition time," when you're waiting for an appointment, standing in line or traveling. Train yourself to read only what's most important to you. Nothing else. Then throw the rest of the magazine away. Ideally, you want to go through the table of contents, circle what's of interest to you and give it to your assistant, who can tear out the pages, put them in a file and shove them into your hands on the way out of the office. **Also, whenever you're reading or reviewing correspondence, stand up! Your mind will stay more focused and alert and you'll get done much faster.**

You may want to take advantage of services that provide a synopsis or overview of various books and articles. Written and audio summaries are available. I've made use of both for several years now and cut out 2 or 3 hours of reading each week.

Vital Time Tactic #4
Handle Everything Once and Only Once

Single handling means once you start a top priority task, stay with it until it's 100 percent complete. Persevere without diversion or distraction. Don't pick up the same task,

Rapid-Fire Time Saver #11

Because you absorb the habits of those you spend time with, associate only with time-conscious people. And, of course, stay away from negative people.

same piece of paper, or even the same phone call twice. Pick it up, swarm all over it, take care of it, then bring it to a close and go on to the next one.

Become a "monomaniac" as Peter Drucker calls it. Learn to focus intensely on just one thing at a time, because the more you take on, the greater the chance that you'll lose some of your effectiveness. This is true not only for a particular task, but in all areas of your life. Research shows that great accomplishments require single-minded concentration. Review the great success stories and you'll see what I mean!

Vital Time Tactic #5
Delegate

Delegation is the only way you can carve out enough Vital Time to pursue those things that are meaningful to you. Without delegation, you will end up with so many responsibilities that you can't do what matters most. Remember, focus on what you do best! As an executive or manager, you must delegate everything you possibly can to have enough time to complete your highest payback tasks. Delegate, and you'll free yourself from mundane tasks that don't move you closer to your goals.

The first step in delegating tasks is to know *when* to delegate. A general rule of thumb is: If someone else can do the job quicker, better, or more economically than you can, get them to do it! **Direct increasing amounts of time to those aspects of your business for which you have the most passion and where you excel.** This is the prescription for exceptional success no matter what you do.

It's been said that activities that don't directly advance your goals and

Rapid-Fire Time Saver #12

Keep note cards or a mini-cassette recorder with you all the time for capturing ideas and dictating letters.

Use the extra time you've freed up to:

• *spend quality and quantity time with those you love*

• *work on important business and career goals and plans*

• *or simply to rest, relax and rejuvenate.*

dreams are simply routine maintenance. And routine maintenance, while critical to the functioning of a house, car, or any piece of machinery, *can be performed by anyone* who has the necessary skills. In other words, by a repair person or a handyman, or someone other than yourself. Unless you want to be a maid, butler, home improvement expert, or auto mechanic, you may be sacrificing hundreds of hours per year on activities that are neither in alignment with your values nor contribute directly to the accomplishment of a single objective, goal, or dream.

You can't be goal-directed and maintenance-directed

at the same time...so make a choice. However, if routine home and yard maintenance are enjoyable for you, then by all means do them! These activities can be effective stress-reducers and can also give you a sense of accomplishment. But if they're not you're idea of a good time, delegate them.

The point here is that *you* make the decision on when to hire someone to take care of the chores *you* consider mundane maintenance. Something you choose to delegate may be very different from what your neighbor or co-worker chooses to delegate. The important thing, however, is that you delegate to someone else those activities that drain your energy and obscure your focus.

It's not only important to decide when to delegate but what to delegate. Giving subordinates jobs that neither you nor anyone else wants to do isn't delegating. It's assigning. And although it's necessary at times, it doesn't nourish their egos, encourage them to grow, or enable them to assume the decision-making role that can help to free more of your time. So learn to delegate the challenging and rewarding tasks as well.

The next important step in delegating is to know who to delegate to. Choose the best people available no matter the cost. *The best people will make you successful.* They also cut down on the number of times you are interrupted because they know how to handle the challenges themselves. The sooner you stop the interruptions at home and in the office, the sooner you'll be living your life *your* way, on *your* terms, and fulfilling *your* goals.

Knowing when to delegate, whom to delegate to, and how to delegate will come more and more naturally with continued practice. You can rest assured it will put you

Rapid-Fire Time Saver #13

Call ahead or fax lunch orders to save waiting in line for take-out orders.

Minimize Telephone Mediocrity

1. Before you call, jot down the points you want to cover.

2. Be prepared to cut the conversation off quickly by reminding the other person of "how busy you know **they** are."

3. Do easy mindless jobs while on the phone like signing letters or organizing your desk.

4. When possible, check your messages and return all necessary calls at the same time. Limit phone usage to a couple of specific periods during the day. You'll immediately become aware of the extra time and mental energy it frees up.

5. Practice the phone management Golden Rule. When you call someone else, value their time by asking, "Is this a good time?" Don't assume they have time to talk to you, and never interrupt simply because you want to chat!

well on your way to claiming and enjoying Vital Time.

Vital Time Tactic #6
Control Your Phone Calls

Control the phone or it will control you and limit your level of accomplishment. Don't be afraid to ignore it completely if you're engaged in a vital activity. Voice mail systems are cost effective and efficient at handling messages, and if you're fortunate enough to have an assistant, have your calls screened. Get a specific call back time when the caller will be in the office. And when you call somebody, leave a call back time as well. Stop phone tag. Refuse to be a slave to the phone.

Another way to control the phone is to become the caller instead of the callee. Research indicates that unplanned phone calls last five to seven minutes longer than planned calls. If you make or receive 12 unplanned calls in a day, that might already be a wasted hour. I have all of my incoming calls carefully screened, which does occasionally irritate some people, but that only warns me that the offended party might be the type of person who can afford to waste time. In my office, under no circumstances are calls put through to me unless the caller fully identifies herself or himself and the reasons for calling. My staff also encourages callers to e-mail or fax me a brief introductory note before trying to get me on the phone. Often, as I've observed, I'm not needed at all.

Rapid-Fire Time Saver #14

Avoid the herd. Do things when nobody else does them. Check out of your hotel when other people aren't. Dine out before crowds arrive. Schedule flights for non-peak hours. Drive during non-peak hours also.

Vital Time Tactic #7
Manage Interruptions

You must become exceptionally skilled at handling interruptions because they tend to be the number

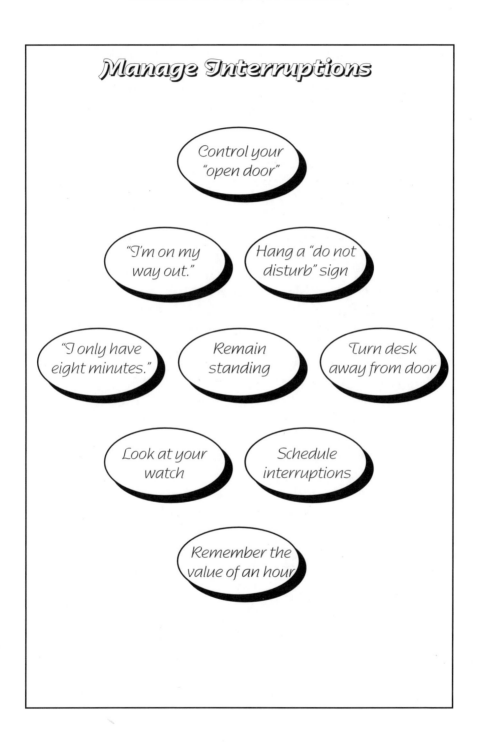

one biggest time waster in business. Remember, interruptions are people — people who want to re-focus your attention from what you're now doing to something else. Some people just don't realize they're being disrespectful, cutting into your time, or disturbing your thought process, while others babble and ramble on indefinitely, apparently believing they're getting paid by the word. They never seem to run out of inconsequential things to say. Either way, here are some strategies for dealing with these time vampires:

• Adapt a controlled open-door policy where people have access to you but by appointment only. **Help develop your staff by requiring them, before they bring you a problem, to clearly define the problem in writing, suggest three possible solutions, and then have them choose and mark the best solution of the three.** Often they'll determine there's no need to interrupt. And if they do interrupt, the length of disruption will be shortened. No one should be able to just walk into your office for whatever reason.

• You could also **designate specific times for interruptions** and other times for no interruptions. Put a hotel "do not disturb" sign on your closed door during these uninterruptable periods or move your work to a conference room or other quiet location. Make it absolutely clear that unless there's a death in the family or there's a fire in the building, you're not to be disturbed. When you do allow interruptions, make sure you're engaged in routine or operational tasks, not creative work.

• When somebody unexpectedly drops in, **stand up and begin to leave**. Just stand up and say, "I'm on my way out" and hold the meeting right there. Then go to the restroom or down the hall, whatever, then get back to work.

Rapid-Fire Time Saver #15

If you're having trouble making contact with someone for the first time on the telephone, consider faxing or e-mailing your message.

Remember the Value of an Hour

Total Annual Income	Total number of hours you work each week				
	30	40	50	60	70
	Approximate $ Value of an Hour of Your Time				
40,000	$26.67	$20.00	$16.00	$13.34	$11.43
45,000	$30.00	$22.50	$18.00	$15.00	$12.86
50,000	$33.34	$25.00	$20.00	$16.67	$14.29
55,000	$36.67	$27.50	$22.00	$18.33	$15.71
60,000	$40.00	$30.00	$24.00	$18.33	$15.71
65,000	$43.33	$32.50	$26.00	$21.67	$18.57
75,000	$50.00	$37.50	$30.00	$25.00	$21.43
100,000	$56.67	$50.00	$40.00	$33.34	$28.57
125,000	$83.33	$62.50	$50.00	$41.67	$35.71
150,000	$100.00	$75.00	$60.00	$50.00	$42.86
200,000	$133.34	$100.00	$80.00	$56.67	$57.14
250,000	$166.67	$125.00	$100.00	$83.33	$71.43
300,000	$200.00	$150.00	$120.00	$100.00	$85.71
350,000	$233.33	$175.00	$140.00	$116.67	$100.00
400,000	$266.67	$200.00	$160.00	$133.34	$114.29
450,000	$300.00	$225.00	$180.00	$150.00	$128.57
500,000	$333.34	$250.00	$200.00	$166.67	$142.86
Total Hours Worked Annually (50 Weeks)	1,500	2,000	2,500	3,000	3,500

To calculate the dollar value of an hour of your time, divide your annual income by the number of hours you work each year.

One hour is worth: $_____

I want one hour to be worth: $_____

• Meet unexpected visitors in the reception area or lobby and remain standing if possible. Meet co-workers in *their* office rather than yours so you can more easily get up and leave when you feel the conversation is over.

• **Set time limits** at the beginning of the discussion. If you have an unexpected guest, say, "I've only got eight minutes, then I've got a phone appointment." Using an unusual time frame catches attention and respect.

• Discourage drop-in visitors by turning your desk away from the door. This eliminates eye contact which some interpret as an invitation for interruption. If someone does drop in, save time when you restart your work by writing down a brief note to remind yourself where you left off.

• **Anxious body language shortens interruptions.** Look at your watch, start to shuffle papers, look for something in your desk, whatever you can think of and the hint will be received. I know some people who always have a mundane task that they ask drop-in visitors to help them with. The more tedious, the better. And again, they'll get the message.

• If your assistant and staff are your most frequent interruptions, **schedule regular blocks of time to meet** and cover all problems and questions in one session.

• Finally, suppose for example that you want to earn $100,000 this year. That translates into approximately $50 an hour or about 83 cents each minute. Keep this fresh in your mind as **most who interrupt others have no clue as to the value of each minute of their time or yours!**

Rapid-Fire Time Saver #16

Batch your errands. Do errands on one side of the street on the way and on the other side on your way back.

Vital Time Tactic #8
Batch Similar Tasks

Do similar things together. Everything we do is subject to what is called the "learning curve." When we

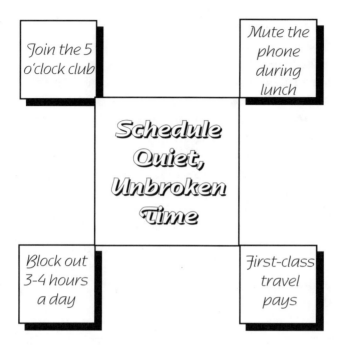

do a series of five to ten similar tasks, the learning curve reduces the amount of time needed to complete each item by about 80 percent.

For instance, in running my business, it's much more productive to set aside certain days for client training, to develop products on another day, and to review research on another day, rather than doing a little bit here, a little bit there, and each time and having to mentally warm up to each type of activity again and again. Batch your phone calls and correspondence as well. Do them all at once and you can add about an hour to your day.

Rapid-Fire Time Saver #17

If you travel a lot, keep a file of directions to places you might return to in your car for handy reference.

Vital Time Tactic #9
Block Out Chunks of Time

You wouldn't believe the feedback I get from entrepreneurs and other leaders on the impact of time blocking. **The more important your work becomes, the more important it becomes for you to develop blocks of time where you can work on serious projects without distraction.** Avoid mixing creative tasks with functional or administrative tasks. In fact, it's impossible to maximize your personal effectiveness if you try to blend operational tasks such as answering the phone, drafting correspondence, and holding meetings, while at the same time trying to work on creative projects such as planning. You need blocks of time. By blocks of time, I mean minimum blocks of two hours on a regular basis. It takes about 30 to 60 minutes for your mind to get acclimated to creative tasks, leaving you with about an hour and a half for productive work.

Here are several recommendations for scheduling quiet, unbroken time. Each will dramatically increase your effectiveness and your efficiency and produce the well-spring of creative ideas that comes from uninterrupted thought.

Rapid-Fire Time Saver #18

Avoid bargainitis or the inflammation of the poverty gland. Bargainitis is simply the practice of false economy. Don't allow cost to be your only criteria. Smart buyers know the concept of "penny-wise and pound foolish" advocated by Ben Franklin still holds true.

• Start off in the morning when you are freshest and most alert. Get up at 5 in the morning. Join the 5 o'clock club. Work on important lifetime priorities, goals, and devotions early in the morning. All great leaders are early risers. After working on personal development, you can devote the rest of your early-morning time to professional projects. This way, you've had 90 minutes of uninterrupted time before you've even

Vital Time Tactics

1. Overcome procrastination

2. Organize your workspace

3. Handle reading material efficiently

4. Handle everything once and only once

5. Delegate

6. Control your phone calls

7. Manage interruptions

8. Batch similar tasks

9. Block out chunks of time

10. Run masterful meetings

gone to the office. Or, you can get into the office an hour or more earlier than anyone else. Even if you get to the office at the usual time, in the 90 minutes of uninterrupted work you've done at home, you could do a half day's work.

• Lunch time is another excellent option for time blocking. From 12 to 1, mute the telephone and while everybody's gone, you can work uninterrupted for more than an hour, clearing up correspondence or tackling chunks of major projects.

• Blocking off a set time every day. For instance, from 10 to 12, put a "do not disturb" sign on the outside of your office door, and for two hours take no interruptions. Between 2 and 4, do the same thing, and you'll get in a solid 2 hours in the morning and the afternoon. The exact times you do this don't really matter. Just do it!

Rapid-Fire Time Saver #19

Experiment with tipping in advance. Remember what TIP stands for: "To Insure Performance" or Promptness. If you're at a nice restaurant and in a hurry, simply tell the person who seats you that you're pressed for time and ask him if he can speed things up in the kitchen. Then slip a bill into his hand and repeat the same maneuver when the server comes. Also, tip generously at any restaurant you frequent. It's an investment!

• Don't overlook travel as an opportunity for time blocking. One hour of first-class air travel, for example, will be the equivalent of about three hours of work in an office environment because there aren't any interruptions. And, it *is* worth the extra investment.

In The 1% Club® we teach entrepreneurs how to block out entire days and, in some cases, even weeks as a focusing tool.*

Vital Time Tactic #10
Run Masterful Meetings

How do your meetings measure up? Are they an investment? Or a waste of time? Here are six essential points for effective meetings.

• **Know the purpose.** Is the goal to solve a problem, to train employ-

*For more information on The 1% Club®, please see the appendix, page 199.

ees, to share information, to plan a project? Be able to define the purpose of the meeting in less than 25 words!

• **Is the meeting absolutely necessary?** Or is there another way to accomplish the same result? Who must attend? What is the worst thing that could happen if the meeting were not held at all? Be aware that most meetings are big time wasters. So view all meetings as investments that should reap large dividends. Multiply the hourly wages of meeting attendees by the number of hours of the meeting to determine the cost.

• **Develop a written agenda.** Provide a copy of meeting topics to participants in advance of the meeting. List the items of discussion in order of importance to the organization. Begin the meeting with a one-sentence statement of purpose, then give the adjournment time.

• **Prepare!** Prepare for the meeting as if it were a client presentation. Always do your homework, and never waste attendees' time with tasks or dialogue that could be handled elsewhere!

• **Lead the meeting effectively.** The leader must keep the meeting on track and state the outcome of each point discussed. Close each point before moving on, and don't skip around. Assign all tasks and deadlines, including the taking and distribution of meeting minutes or notes. Determine how each task discussed in the meeting will be implemented and controlled. Be absolutely clear on what is to be done *and* why, and have employees re-state the task, the deadline, and the purpose to make sure everyone understands what's going on. Above all, make decisions. Meetings without decisions are worthless.

• **Get out fast.** Leave if you are

Rapid-Fire Time Saver #20

Create checklists for recurring activities like home maintenance, car maintenance, house cleaning, vacation planning, and grocery shopping. You won't have to re-think it each time the need arises.

no longer necessary for the completion of the meeting. Try to get items affecting you discussed first, and then leave and get back to work! Leaders should give their people permission to depart after their contribution has been made.

We all have just 24 hours each day to achieve our goals and to become the person we are capable of becoming. Like I said at the beginning of this lesson, no matter who you are, your progress and ultimate success in life will depend more on what you do with the 24 hours you're given each day than on any other single factor. You can invest your time wisely or you can waste it foolishly! Create Vital Time or let it slip away! The choice, as always, is yours! It's completely up to you!

Rapid-Fire Time Saver #21

Do things right the first time. If you don't have time to do it right the first time, when will you have time to re-do it?

Lesson 4
<u>Assignments</u>

1. Determine how much your time is currently worth (see chart on page 99).

2. Determine how much your time *should* be worth to create the lifestyle you desire.

3. Make a list of your top 3 highest payback activities, both personally and professionally.

4. Keep a log of your time for the next 2 weeks. (Use 15-minute increments.)

5. Based on this lesson, brainstorm a list of 20 ways you can specifically improve your personal time management.

Lesson 5

Choose to Get Out of Your Own Way

Whatever you direct your mind to think about will ultimately be revealed for everyone to see.

Learn the Language of Success

Flush Unwanted Dialogue Out Of Your Mind

Control Your Emotions

Build Beliefs That Make Success Inevitable

Get Out of Your Own Way

Re-program Yourself For Extraordinary Accomplishment

*A*mong the most powerful influences on your character, personality, and attitude is what you say to yourself and what you believe. At every single moment of every day, you are either talking yourself into or out of success. By talking yourself into success, I mean talking yourself into your unique definition of success. Remember our discussion in Lesson One. You are constantly redefining and reinventing yourself and your future with every thought that races through your mind. It's a scientific fact that we are constantly talking to ourselves, and this inner dialogue, or self-talk, can and must be controlled if we are to maximize our God-given potential.

What is Self-Talk?

Self-talk can be most simply defined as what you say or think to yourself, either silently or aloud. Silent self-talk is commonly referred to as your thoughts, but it's actually a silent conversation that you hold in the privacy of your own mind. You *are* thinking all the time, day and night, 24 hours a day. In fact, psychologists estimate that the average person thinks between 20,000 and 60,000 thoughts per day. Every thought you think either moves you toward your goals and the person you hope to become, or it moves you away. No thoughts are neutral. Every thought counts. Unfortunately, approximately 90 percent of the thoughts you have today are repeats from yesterday and the day before, and the day before that. This is the primary reason why effecting permanent, positive improvement in your life tends to be such an uphill challenge. The human mind loves the status quo and, if not trained otherwise, it will feed you a constant repetition of old ideas. Those old thoughts, like an automatic pilot, will keep steering your life in the same direction it has always gone.

On page 112 are some common examples of what people speak out loud or say to themselves silently:

How to Talk Yourself
Out of Success

- *I can never remember his name.*
- *I just always seem to dip into my savings.*
- *Shoot, I lost my train of thought.*
- *I can never say that right.*
- *You can't teach an old dog new tricks.*
- *You can't have your cake and eat it, too.*
- *I just know my limitations.*
- *I'm just this way.*
- *I'm losing my mind.*
- *That makes me sick.*
- *Just my luck...*
- *That's out of my price range. I can't afford it.*
- *I don't have enough time.*
- *The ones I like, don't like me, and the ones who like me, well, there's always something wrong with them.*
- *That's too rich for my blood.*
- *If I had money, I'd just worry about losing it.*
- *I'm living proof of Murphy's Laws.*
- *I'll never understand those types of things.*
- *Everything I eat goes straight to my waist.*
- *Nobody wants to pay me what I'm worth.*
- *I used to have so much energy.*
- *My metabolism is slowing down.*
- *If such and such happens, I'm going to be sooo mad.*

Pay attention to almost any conversation for about eight or ten minutes and you'll hear the toxic self-talk, the whining, complaining, blaming, condemning, and justifying.

As King Solomon put it several thousand years ago, "As a man thinketh in his heart, so is he!"

You'll hear people passionately arguing in favor of their most cherished limitations, and you'll also hear them knocking, sometimes in a subtle manner, those who have overcome those same limitations and done far more with their lives. Some insist that they're not being negative, just realistic, giving you an honest description of how their lives are right now. But ignorance of the law is no excuse. Where you've been and what you've done matters far less than where you're going. **But if you persist in constantly identifying with current or prior performance by thinking and talking about it, then where you've been, where you are, and where you're going will all be one and the same.** This holds true for your golf game, your business career, your marriage, and every other area of your life.

Become a Visionary

The purpose of this lesson is to help you become a visionary with your life, someone who can sense things as they could be rather than just as they are. Someone who acknowledges the sun when only clouds are visible. This is a vital skill which is in short supply, and when you master it, you can create opportunities for yourself and for others that most people won't even accept as a possibility.

Imagine some part of your life that you'd like to improve. It could be a personal quality, a habit, an attitude, a financial problem, a challenge with your weight, or any other area of dissatisfaction. Since this area of dissatisfaction is below your standards, consider yourself to be down in a hole, far beneath your potential. It doesn't matter so much how you got in the hole — just that you're aware that you're in the hole. To get out, you're going to have to think *up*, look *up*, speak *up* and ultimately climb *up*. Remember this as the first rule of holes: If you're in one, stop digging. Most people have difficulty climbing out of the holes in their lives simply because they focus more on the hole (which represents their current circumstance), than on where they want to climb (which is the goal or solution). They are slowed down, weighed down, and bogged down in reality. And they'll keep getting more of what they've already gotten.

You must make the shift from reactive thinking to proactive thinking. You must stop working for your mind and instead, enlist your mind to work for you. Remember, your self-talk tends to work against you unless you are aware of it and use it for your own goals and ambitions. So, for the rest of this lesson I will use the phrase "self-talk" to refer to **positive** self-talk. **Positive self-talk is a thought you intentionally choose to think because of the results it will produce in your life.** It is a positive, assertive, present tense description of a goal or other desired condition. It describes your lifestyle as it will be when you have achieved your goals.

A belief is a collection of subconscious thoughts which represent what you consider to be the absolute truth about any given situation or condition in your life. It's a feeling of absolute certainty. Your beliefs are literally hardwired, primarily through repetition, into neural pathways within your brain. Incoming data from your senses travels along these pathways on its way to interpretation in the brain. This means that prior to interpretation by your brain, incoming data from your senses is filtered

How We Cling
to Limiting Beliefs

1. We **make life choices that harmonize** with our beliefs. We unconsciously choose situations and people that fit our preconceptions while avoiding those people and situations that might weaken or contradict our beliefs. We also display emotions, body language, and facial expressions that attract situations that match up with our beliefs.

2. We practice **selective attention** or inattention depending on the circumstance. Our minds tune in to phenomena that confirm our beliefs while avoiding, ignoring, or deleting anything that could weaken the belief. We selectively remember events that fit our beliefs and selectively forget those that do not.

3. We automatically **distort**, mold, or exaggerate evidence to reasonably fit our belief.

4. We may also, as a last ditch effort, **rationalize contradictory evidence** to uphold a belief. Often this is a misinterpretation of motives for an action or the claiming of an ulterior motive.

through your beliefs. Reality is therefore not fixed but manipulated by our beliefs.

Self-talk represents specific mental energy which is received by the brain, then is downloaded into neurological tracks and processed to create the actions we take. **You are not consciously aware of most of your beliefs because you have been living with them for so long.** As a result, beliefs are like "assumed truths" that need not be questioned. And if you never question or challenge a belief, it sticks with you forever, becoming an ever stronger conviction.

Typically, people will do just about anything to keep their beliefs intact, even if it's a damaging or self-defeating belief. Since replacing a limiting or erroneous belief requires a combination of curiosity, humility, and courage, it's a rare occurrence. Many limiting beliefs also exonerate us from taking action and pursuing opportunities, from leaving our comfort zone or taking on greater responsibility. Still other limiting beliefs provide us with convenient alibis for doing less work.

What is Reality?

It's important to remember that what we perceive as reality is not necessarily "true" or "actual" reality at all, but only our personal version of reality. **We get only an edited look at the world around us.** This is because our beliefs, for better or for worse, act as filters, screening out any evidence that doesn't support our belief. We screen reality through our senses, our language, our inborn tendencies, and especially, through generalizations we make relative to our personal experiences. It is in this fourth category of screens, the generalizations we make relative to our personal experiences, where we can make a substantial impact with positive self-talk. The beliefs that make up your self-concept come from the generalizations, many of them self-defeating, you have made throughout your life. In a number of different ways, we tend to cling to our limiting beliefs like a child to his security blanket, even when there is evidence to the contrary.

The reason our subconscious goes to so much trouble to maintain our beliefs lies in the nature of the beast. Human beings have an unconscious tendency to continue doing what they've always done, to remain consistent with

what they've said and done in the
past. Any attempt to change
current habits of
thought or ac-
tion triggers
the homeo-
static impulse
which makes
you feel uneasy
and uncomfort-
able. Since the hu-
man brain seeks

> Successful men and women train their minds to think only about what they want to happen in their lives.

comfort and pleasure, and tries to avoid and move away
from discomfort and pain, your natural tendency will be
to go back to the old ways of doing things. While this tendency is natural and common, it must be overcome if you
are to unlock your full potential. You must be willing to be
uncomfortable or uneasy if you want the rewards of higher
levels of personal effectiveness.

The Mental Principles

To fully benefit from self-talk it is helpful to understand
the seven mental principles that support them. Principles,
by definition, are timeless. They are in effect for everyone,
everywhere, 24 hours a day. Just as physical laws do not
discriminate, neither do the following mental laws:

1. Cause and Effect. For every single effect in your
life, there is a cause or group of causes. If you want to
produce a specific result in your life you must trace back
from that result and identify the cause or causes. The most
important application of this principle is that **your
thoughts are causes and your circumstances are effects.**
In other words, all causation is mental. Nothing happens
by accident. And just because a cause can not be determined does not mean there is no cause. However, many do

attribute the effects in their lives, the results they achieve, to either good or bad luck. This is done for one of three reasons: (1) to relieve the individual from a sense of responsibility if it's bad luck, which deflects attention from the true source, (2) to appear modest or humble if the luck is good, or (3) simple ignorance as to the true cause or causes.

2. Belief. The principle of belief says that whatever you believe long enough and hard enough becomes true for you. According to your beliefs it is done unto you. Whatever you tell yourself repeatedly with feeling you come to believe. You do not so much believe what you see as you see what you've *already* decided to believe. **Your beliefs produce life experiences, not the other way around.** Once a belief is locked in, you tend to notice only those things which reinforce or create additional evidence that your belief is true. This selective perception allows you to create and experience your own personal version of reality.

3. Subconscious activity. Any emotionally charged thought or idea that is repeatedly held in your conscious mind is interpreted as a command by your subconscious mind. Since the subconscious mind cannot distinguish between truth and fantasy, it accepts verbal input without regard to present reality. In effect, the subconscious is a perfect servant. It always agrees with and complies with what the conscious mind tells it. It becomes like a parrot, repeating and replaying the commands you've given it. **Your job is to convince the subconscious that the condition you desire already exists.** Your subconscious then piques your awareness to the opportunities around you that are consistent with your goals. You will attract into your life the ideas, events, and circumstances that harmonize with your most dominant self-talk.

4. Substitution. The conscious mind can hold only one thought at a time, either positive or negative. But you cannot eliminate a thought directly. You can do so only by substituting another one for it. If I say to you, "Don't think of a pink elephant," you, of course, immediately think of it. If you say, "I refuse to think of a pink elephant," then you're still thinking about it. If you tell

Whatever you direct your mind to think about will ultimately be revealed for everyone to see.

someone to not worry, it's a very difficult task because you can't concentrate on the reverse of something. It's not possible. But if you give them something else specific to think about, then the new thought displaces the current thought. Thoughts of worry are replaced with thoughts of faith and confidence. Thoughts of boldness replace thoughts of fear. You can get rid of that pink elephant with a big white horse. This is the principle of substitution. You *can* exert control over your thinking and, by extension, your life, by replacing any negative, counterproductive thoughts with positive, empowering thoughts.

5. Mental Equivalency. Before physical creation there has to be a mental creation. This means that you must develop a clear, vivid mental picture of any goal you hope to achieve *in advance* of its actual accomplishment. Before you can have something new and different in your life, before you can have something new and different on the outside, you must become new and different on the inside or in the way you think. You must be willing to let go of the old you to make room for the new you. You must be willing to shake yourself free of your old ways of thinking and doing if you truly desire a new and improved life experience. Positive self-talk strengthens your mental equivalent, causing it to become a powerful magnetic force, attracting into your life exactly what you need to reach your goals.

6. Concentration. The principle of concentration states that whatever you focus upon grows and expands. You will be effective to the degree that you can concentrate single-mindedly on only one thing and stick with it until it's complete. If you dwell upon your positive experiences, your blessings, your goals, and all the people who love you, then you will attract even more blessings, even more love, and even more accomplishments. The more you emphasize your good health, the healthier you feel. The more you emphasize and dwell upon the positive qualities in your spouse, the stronger your relationship will become. This works for good or for bad, so be careful where you place your mental priorities. Whatever you stop thinking about or turn your attention away from tends to fall out of your life. So refuse to entertain thoughts of doubt, fear, or worry. See if you can go 24 hours without a hint of fear, criticism or negativity of any kind in your thoughts and conversations. You can build any virtue into your mentality by dwelling upon that virtue every single day. So choose to think about good things!

7. Relaxation. Trying too hard mentally actually becomes counterproductive. Mental effort tends to defeat itself. In the physical world, though, the harder you work, the faster you progress. The harder you work at digging a hole in the ground, the sooner you'll have a ditch. The harder you hammer a nail, the faster it penetrates a 2-by-4. **But when you try to force things mentally, or press, as it's referred to by athletes, your mind freezes up and stops working creatively.** This generally produces more of what you don't want. Your subconscious absorbs positive self-talk fastest when you are relaxed and unhurried. Thoughts of worry, fear, anxiety, or doubt are all signs of mental struggle that must be eliminated. But wrestling with an unwanted thought just injects it with more power. Instead, calmly and gently replace it with any positive or constructive idea and the negative thought will fade away. Prac-

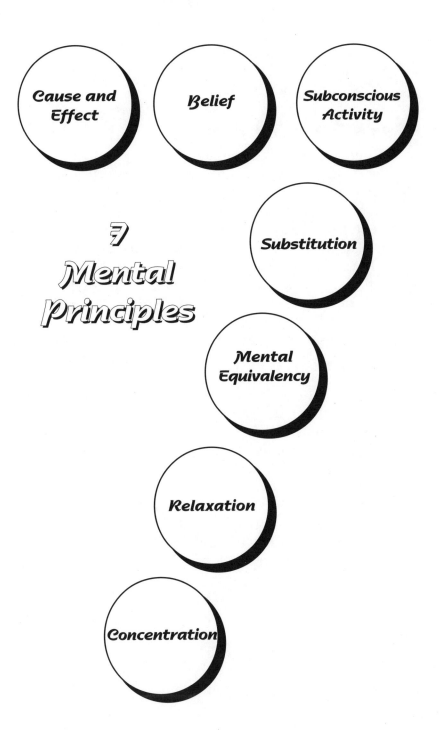

Cause and Effect

Belief

Subconscious Activity

7 Mental Principles

Substitution

Mental Equivalency

Relaxation

Concentration

tice blending your self-talk with a calm sense of positive expectancy, the feeling and "knowing" that everything is working out in your favor.

The P.E.P.P. Formula

Effective self-talk is created by using the P.E.P.P. formula: Positively phrased, Emotion provoking, Present tense and Personal.

Use specific, precise, **positively phrased** language in your self-talk. Say, "I am reading for one hour every evening," rather than, "I am no longer wasting my evenings watching TV." Instead of affirming, "I am not eating ice cream," say, "I am eating only low-fat, nutritious foods." Rather than programming yourself not to get sick, program yourself to stay healthy and vibrant. Since your mind thinks in pictures, it has difficulty processing a negatively stated goal. It's impossible for your mind to create a picture of yourself *not* doing something. Stating self-talk positively also shifts your concentration from what you don't want to what you do want.

Next, your self-talk should be **emotion provoking**, causing you to pre-live the experience. The more feeling you blend with your self-talk, the more and faster it impacts the subconscious. Experiment with using bold words that are fun and passionate. Use words you haven't used much before. Break the verbal rut. Also try adding "feeling" words such as easily, joyfully, effortlessly, boldly, or gratefully into your self-talk statements.

The next P is for **present tense**. Your self-talk should always be in the present tense. The subconscious mind, where permanent change becomes rooted, does not understand or acknowledge the past or the future. It operates only in the here and now. You can effect subconscious change only by communicating in the language it understands, the present tense. This comes from the theory of cognitive dissonance, which states that when you hold two psychologically inconsistent thoughts, you experience dissonance, or a sense of tension and inharmonious feelings. The subconscious, in an attempt to reduce the discomfort of the conflicting messages, does everything it can to create the most recently imposed suggestion or self-talk. Repetition of a specific self-talk statement narrows the gap between conflicting conscious and subconscious beliefs. With persistent repetition, old neurological grooves are erased and replaced, creating, in effect, upgraded mental software. Your subconscious computer then supplies you with the words, actions, mannerisms, body language, creativity, emotions, and other responses consistent with the most dominant mental images imprinted on the brain. Initially, this can feel a bit unusual or uncomfortable because

Positively phrased

Emotion provoking

Present tense

Personal

you are, in effect, speaking about the future as if it's already here. Since this is not the typical way most of us learned to communicate, it's bound to feel strange. Just accept that this is how your mind works. When you affirm your goals and dreams as if they're already attained, you make the shift from being bogged down in reality to being a visionary. **The most powerful words in the English language are those that come after the words "I am."**

The last P is for **personal**. Self-talk you design yourself, that is personal to your life and your goals, is most effective. When you begin, it's often helpful to borrow self-talk from other sources, and then make edits to personalize them, even though you'll experience the strongest connection to the self-talk you've composed yourself. However, any self-talk repeated often enough will be internalized and become part of your unique mental makeup.

Formulating Your Own Self-Talk

Since everything you think or say should lead to the accomplishment of your goals, you must have a definite and specific idea of what your most important life goals are. In addition, you should have complete clarity about why those goals are important to you and how you're going to accomplish them — the action plan! So before attempting to create your own self-talk, invest the time and mental effort, as discussed in Lessons 2 and 3, to get really clear on the What, the Why, and the How. After you've determined the results you're striving for, imagine you've already achieved those results. See yourself as already in possession of your most important goals. Just think *as if*. Really experience the satisfaction and sense of accomplishment. Now, ask yourself this key question: "If I had already accomplished these goals, what would I believe about myself that I don't now truly believe?" Make a list of the thoughts that come to your mind. What would you believe about yourself, your abilities, your mental toughness, your habits, your potential? What would you believe about your lifestyle? What would you believe about the world? Answering these questions is how you develop the mindset of the person you must become if you truly want to reach your goals. Before you can have, you must do, but before you can do you must become. And if you don't lay the foundation of becoming the right person, then whatever you achieve will certainly slip away. It will not, in fact, it cannot be permanent.

If becoming financially independent were your goal, then your answers to the question of "Why haven't you already...?" may have sounded something like this:

- *I'm too young to be financially independent.*
- *I didn't start planning soon enough.*
- *I don't deserve it yet.*
- *I need to get into another field.*
- *I'm not up on good investment strategies.*
- *My goals weren't set high enough.*
- *I think it takes about 30 years to get rich.*
- *I still waste too much time on paperwork.*
- *I've got too many family expenses right now.*
- *Taxes are too high.*
- *Interest rates are too low.*
- *And so on…*

Here's another technique for clarifying your beliefs: Think of one of the most compelling goals you want to achieve in the next three years. Develop a clear picture of it in your mind. Now answer this simple but profound question: Why don't you have it already? If your goal is to be financially independent and that's very important to you, then why aren't you already financially independent? Why haven't you already accomplished this goal? Think of the possible answers for your specific goal. Whatever answers you come up with, whether they be logical, factual, mathematical or whether they be exaggerations, distortions, fears, or other excuses of the imagination, they are still real as far as the accomplishment of your goal is concerned. Every answer you came up with, whether factual or fictional, represents a limited belief or a blind spot in your mental equivalent. Self-talk helps you shore up your mental equivalent. It gives you the ability to create and fortify beliefs that support the person you want to become and the goals you want to achieve.

Simply create self-talk statements which represent something close to the opposite of the limiting belief. For example:

- *I'm too young to become financially independent becomes: I am the perfect age to enjoy financial independence.*

- *I still waste too much time on paperwork becomes: I focus on new business generation and delegate everything else.*

- *I don't deserve it yet becomes: I am ready for and worthy of financial independence right now!*

Whatever your answers were, it doesn't matter. You can turn any of them to your advantage by practicing **positive opposite therapy**, which activates the principle of substitution.

Positive opposite therapy provides you with the mental nourishment that must come before goal achievement. If you dwell on the right beliefs, they will take root and multiply into strong convictions which will override and smother old negative beliefs. You can best deploy your mental energies by focusing on where you want to go rather than where you are and where you've been. Remember, you can and do, either intentionally or haphazardly, determine what you believe. What you choose to believe is completely up to you. The important question is this: "What should you believe?" We know that beliefs come first and results come second. So, what should you believe? An accurate answer to this question requires that you first develop complete clarity about your future. The clearer your vision for the future is, the easier it will be to determine what you must first believe in order to get there.

The Person You Must Become

When formulating your self-talk, consider the skills that you need to develop, the habits, knowledge and attitude that you need, the virtues you may need before you reach the goal, the different qualities you may need, and the belief systems that need to be in place. Ask yourself, "What sort of person do I need to be before I can achieve these goals?"

Composing your own self-talk forces you to look at the accomplishment of your goals from all angles. So ask yourself, "What skills do I need to develop?" Then, when you've determined those skills, turn them into a self-talk statement. For example, to develop communication skills, constantly affirm: I communicate effectively, I listen well and I ask good questions. Same thing with habits. Determine the habits you need to develop, the things you need to do regularly to become the person you've described and to reach the goals you want to achieve, then affirm that you already have that habit, affirm that you already have the knowledge you need, affirm that you already have all the qualities, characteristics, virtues, and attitudes in place *in advance* of the accomplishment of your goals. Think as if you're already the person you want to become. Also, as you're formulating your self-talk statements, use the word "now" as much as possible. Of course, all of your self-talk statements should be in the present tense, but either at the beginning of the statement or near the end, just add the word "now." "I am now achieving goals faster than ever before." "I accept myself completely right now." Also, experiment with using "ing" words, action words such as "doing, achieving, accomplishing, winning, creating, finding, helping, loving..." Using those words in your self-talk statements helps you to get the feeling and to imagine yourself already in possession of the goal. And the majority of your self-talk statements should start with either the words "I" or "my." I have also found that the following phrases are particularly helpful in almost any self-talk. Use as many of them as you want in developing your own self-talk statements:

Expect	Ready for	Prepared	Open to
Accept	Receive	Love	Comfortable with
Allow	Worthy of	Willing	Deserve

Decide what you want to create in your life, then plug these key words into your self-talk statements. Relentlessly repeat that you **expect** to reach your goals — that you're **ready for** it, **prepared for** it, **open to** it, that you **accept** it into your life, that you now **receive** it, that you're **comfortable with** it. Repeatedly affirm that you are **worthy** of your goal, that you **love** it, and that you **deserve** it, and

finally, that you're **willing** to do
whatever it takes to reach
it. The nature of
these authori-
tative
com-
mands re-
duces the
psychologi-
cal resistance
to change and
helps prevent a

*Many people say things to them-
selves that they would never, ever
say to a respected friend.
Be a respected friend to yourself.
Be a nourishing friend to yourself.*

retreat to the comfort zone. So bombard yourself with
thoughts like these. Drive them into your mind so that they
penetrate the subconscious. To receive a free set of self-
talk cards to help you, please see the appendix, page 209.

Strengthen Your Mind

Remember, all of life is an exercise in strengthening
your mind. A flabby mind allows a continuous stream of
thoughts swirling at 100 miles per hour, never channeled
in a single direction for any length of time. Every thought
you have or word you speak triggers an image consistent
with it. Then, like operating instructions, those images act
on you. So make the inner shift from taking commands to
giving commands, to becoming a deliberate and purposeful thinker. Like anything else, with practice, winning self-
talk will become a reflex. You'll begin to consistently amaze
yourself and others.

Silent Talk

There are several ways to deliberately use self-talk. The
first is silent talk, taking control of the thoughts that occupy your mind. Simply repeat specific self-talk statements
over and over to yourself. Think what you want to think
about. This serves several purposes. First, it keeps you fo-

cused on your goals, on what you want versus what you don't want. Second, silent talk trains your mind to think purposefully instead of randomly. You become a proactive thinker, rather than a reactive thinker. These silent conversations then gradually become your habitual thinking pattern. What began as a challenging attempt to improve your thinking becomes an effortless and highly productive mental habit. The third benefit of silent talk is that it interrupts and blocks out stale, self-defeating thinking through substitution.

Verbalization

Verbalization, or audible self-talk, serves the same purpose as silent talk but is considerably more persuasive and powerful. Anything you say aloud with passion and conviction has twice the impact of what you say quietly to yourself. This is because you're involving more of your brain by using more of your senses. The more senses you involve, the faster your self-talk is internalized and absorbed by your subconscious. And the quicker you internalize, the quicker you improve. By hearing yourself speak the thought, you complete what psycholinguists call the language loop. This creates a double reinforcement because *your* ears hear *your* voice giving the order. So repeat your self-talk like you really mean it. Go for loudness if that stirs up more emotion. Shout your self-talk. Remember, you're in charge of delivering operating instructions to your subconscious. If you don't do it, someone else will. You can count on it. Just do what you have to do to get the message across. The most important person for you to impress is yourself. And if you convince yourself, you can convince the world.

If you're just getting started with audible self-talk, you may want to experiment with it privately at first. If you drive solo to work in the morning, that's a wonderful time to shout your self-talk aloud. You'll get your day off to a powerful start and avoid the poison of morning radio. You might even break the monotony of the morning commute and bring a smile to the face of other drivers who spot you chatting with yourself. Verbalizing in the shower is another easy way to prepare for an extraordinary day. Even sing your self-talk. Just make up songs that affirm the reality you want to create. Everybody has a good voice in the shower.

Mirror Talk

If you're willing to feel a little uncomfortable at first, you will find that mirror talk generates an intense emotional reaction. The way to do it is this: Choose one specific self-talk command to practice and then go stand confidently and erect in front of a mirror, preferably a full-length mirror, and make good eye contact with yourself. It's been said that the eyes are the window to the soul and after you try this method you'll realize just what that means. Look deeply into your eyes and repeat your self-talk aloud and with as much feeling as possible. Recite your single, specific command 50 to 100 times and resist the urge to break eye contact. This technique often produces an invigorating emotional reaction, particularly with self-talk concerning your self-esteem and self-worth. With many people, a surge of undiscovered subconscious negativity rises to the surface. This is actually vitally important because uncovering limiting and destructive beliefs is the first step to eliminating them. If you doubt the effectiveness of this method, try it just before you go to sleep, affirming with enthusiasm, "I am alert with boundless energy! I am alert with boundless energy!" while looking into your eyes in front of a mirror. Then see if you can drift right to sleep.

Partner Talk

In partner talk, you provide a trusted friend with a set of self-talk statements phrased in the second person. For example, your partner might affirm to you: "You are lean, muscular, and confident. You believe in yourself. You earn $100,000 in annual income." Your partner speaks affirmations to you and you accept each affirmation by responding, "Yes, I am," or, "Yes, I do, thank you." Then switch roles and do the same for your partner. Remember, what other people say to you strongly influences your self-image. Permanent improvement on the outside comes only after you improve your self-image. And when used intentionally, suggestions from others, or hetero-suggestion, can powerfully override old data and reinforce new, positive habits of thought and behavior. A more casual variation of this method is to get a friend or your spouse to affirm to you each time you see or speak to each other that you already have a particular quality or have already accomplished a specific goal. Since your subconscious mind processes positive assertive statements about you from others as if they were a fact, there is no limit to the progress you can make. Repeated suggestions from others tend to carry a lot of weight.

Self-Conversation

Self-conversation is an advanced form of subconscious programming that requires you to hold down both ends of a conversation. Self-conversation works well because it most closely resembles the continuous unconscious inner dialogue you have with yourself. Your habitual inner dialogue consists of repeated question and answer sessions that are often stimulated by your environmental exposures and circumstances. In other words, your inner dialogue tends to be a random, reactive dialogue rather than purposeful. The question-answer format is the brain's way of evaluating your experiences. To practice self-conversation, write a series of important questions concerning your character and your goals along with the corresponding answers to each of the questions. The aim of this exercise is to determine and then to crystallize the most perfect response

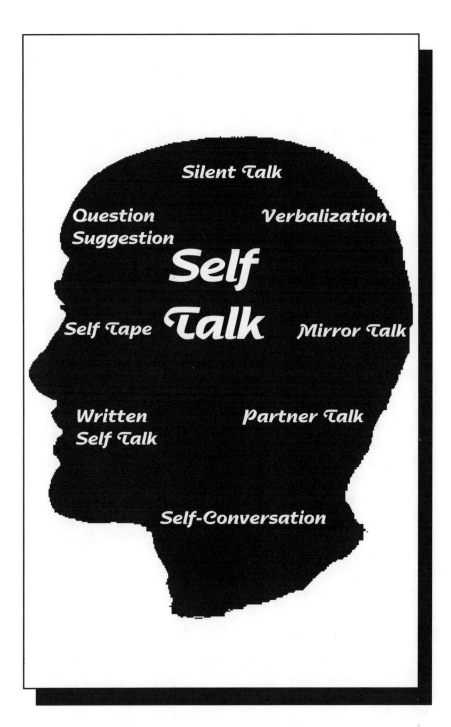

to each of the questions. How would you like to be able to answer each of the questions? An easy way to organize your self-conversation is to use note cards. Take six to ten note cards, and on one side write the important question. On the other side write the answer you desire. This should be your ideal answer. Read the questions and corresponding answers several times a day. This can be done either silently or aloud. Repeated use of this technique trains your mind to entertain only empowering inner dialogues, conversations that lead you in positive directions. You get in the habit of asking better questions and giving better answers. You control the inner dialogue rather than it controlling you. Here's an example of what might be on the question side of one of your note cards: "Good morning, How are you doing today?" The answer you write is up to you but it might go something like this: "I'm doing terrific this morning. I got just the right amount of sleep and I'm raring to go. I'm clear about my goals and what I must do to reach them. I expect the best of myself and others today and that's exactly what I'm going to get."

Your note cards should include a mix of specific goal-related questions along with more general attitudinal or character type questions. The answer you give is really just self-talk in response to a particular question. This method works because the question tends to make your subconscious more receptive to the self-talk or answer. It conditions the soil, so to speak. This method is fun and effective if you can move beyond the often initial feeling of silliness or embarrassment. You'll begin to notice a subtle change in your outlook, habits, and what you say when you talk to yourself. For extra effect, have your partner ask you the question instead.

Written Self-Talk

Written self-talk is the consistent practice of writing and rewriting your goals and supportive self-talk statements. Rewriting your self-talk is a psycho-neural muscular activity which helps align your subconscious beliefs with your conscious goals. Each time you rewrite your self-talk it becomes more clear and more

Whatever you emphasize consciously gets impressed subconsciously.

real. Writing involves thinking of a desired outcome, the act of actually printing it on paper, and then scanning or reviewing it when finished. It forces you to integrate several senses toward the same result, which expedites the internalization of the self-talk. Your written, present tense description activates your reticular cortex, the portion of your brain that determines what you notice and are aware of. **Each time you rewrite your self-talk, you become increasingly more alert to the people, ideas, information, and resources that can help you achieve your goals.** And since you think approximately 20,000 to 60,000 thoughts per day, the *rewriting* of five to ten of these thoughts or affirmations on a regular basis causes your mind to interpret what keeps getting rewritten as having more importance or significance. As a result, your awareness will be heightened concerning those self-talk commands. You become hypersensitive to what moves you toward your goal and what does not. Whatever you emphasize consciously gets impressed subconsciously. Whatever you express becomes impressed. Since you think in pictures, be sure to print your self-talk in bold, block letters. This gives your brain a crisp, clear, and distinct image to absorb. It also takes longer to print, forcing you to be still, concentrate and think more deeply about the person you want to become and the goals you want to achieve. Simultaneously writing and reading your self-talk affects you at a very deep level like a double dose of energy.

Written self-talk is effective anytime, but especially first thing in the morning and right before you go to sleep. These are the two periods (within about 15 minutes after waking and 15 minutes prior to falling asleep) that your brain wave activity slows down and puts you in a highly suggestive or programmable state. Written self-talk channels your attention toward what's most important and away from what's least important. It doesn't have to take any more than four to eight minutes, and you'll find it's an inspiring and refreshing way to start and end each day. Feel free to revise your self-talk as you go if you think of better ways to express it.

Rewriting your goals on a regular basis may also help you discover or uncover any conflicting beliefs you have about a particular goal. Constantly rewriting your goals tends to become a positive addiction if your goals are right for you. On the other hand, if a goal is not right for you, you'll tend to develop an aversion to constantly rewriting it, almost like a body rejects an incompatible organ. This is a valuable clue that you might be on the wrong path and it may save you months or even years of frustrated effort.

Self-Tape

Self-tape is the recording of your personal self-talk in your own voice onto an audio recorder. This is an easy and effortless way to reprogram yourself by listening to yourself repeatedly giving positive commands. To make your own self-tape, choose ten to twelve positively phrased statements that support your goals. Remember the P.E.P.P. formula. Make your self-tape positive, emotion provoking, present tense, and personal. You can concentrate on one area of life for all twelve statements or you can divide them among different areas of life. I prefer to specialize by concentrating on one area of life per tape or at least per side of the tape. Once you've decided on the self-talk statements, you'll need a recorder and a CD player to provide background music. Classical tends to work best, helping you to relax and absorb as you listen, but any type of relaxing instrumental music will do. Read your self-talk into the recorder as the music plays in the background. Repeat each of your statements three to five times before moving to the next one. Also, it's a good idea to alternate between a strong command voice, a relaxed statement, and whispers. The first round of self-talk should be present tense, first-person statements. Keep repeating the cycle of self-talk as needed depending on the length of the tape. You may also want to repeat the cycle in the second person as if someone else is affirming to you. For example: "You are goal directed." Listen to your tape as often as possible. Remember, it's not important that you always pay close attention. If you can hear it, you'll be gaining a benefit. You may also want to record a present tense description of your ideal day, your personal mission statement or any important event you'll be involved in.

Question Suggestion

The last self-talk method is what I call question suggestion, an indirect and subtle technique for programming your subconscious mind. Question suggestion is the deliberate process of asking and re-asking yourself specific questions which presuppose the conditions and circumstances you desire. To help you better understand, let me first give you some common examples of negative suggestive questions.

Negative Suggestive Questions

- *Why can't I ever lose that last five pounds?*
- *Why am I always so tired when I wake up?*
- *How did I get to be so clutzy?*
- *Why do I always dip into my savings?*
- *Why am I never given the credit I deserve?*
- *Why do I always sell myself short?*

What made the above questions negative and self-limiting is that they were so structured that they actually assumed, or took for granted, the unwanted condition. If you ask, "How did I get to be so clutzy?" you're first of all assuming that you are, in fact, a clutz rather than just somebody who in the past has acted clutzy. Second, you're commanding your subconscious to manufacture evidence which supports your assumption. In other words, you're setting in motion a disappointing self-fulfilling prophecy. Remember, your subconscious obediently complies with the directives you or others give it. Watch out for the presumptive questions of those you live and work with. Are their questions helping or hurting you?

Question suggestion is a tool that helps you take conscious control of the questions you repeatedly ask yourself. Your thinking can only be as good as the questions you repeatedly ask, so ask questions which direct your attention and awareness to the best things in your life. Ask questions that challenge your creativity and potential. Ask possibility questions. Ask questions that bring out the best in you. Here are some examples:

Bring Out the Best

- *Aren't I fortunate to be so healthy?*

- *Aren't I fortunate to have tons of energy?*

- *How can I be even more productive today and enjoy the process?*

- *What will happen this week that will bring me total pleasure and satisfaction?*

- *I wonder how many lives I will positively impact today?*

- *Isn't it great that I'm always in the right place at the right time?*

The above questions are empowering because they assume or take for granted a positive desired condition or outcome. When I asked, "Aren't I fortunate to be so healthy," the suggestion or command is: You are already so healthy. That's how the brain interprets it. When I asked, "Isn't it great that I'm always in the right place at the right time," I was really programming myself to be in the right place at the right time. When I asked, "Aren't I fortunate to have tons of energy," I was claiming and affirming that I *already* had tons of energy.

You'll find that questions immediately change what you're focusing on and, consequently, how you feel, how creative you are, how excited you are and how motivated you are at any given moment.

Aren't you fortunate to be reading this lesson?

15 *Practical Insights*

Here are 15 key ideas or insights that will help you talk yourself into even more success and get the most out of this lesson.

1. Always use the word "when" rather than "if" in situations where you are talking about something you want to happen. Say, "when I close that sale," or, "when I lose that weight," I'm going to take a day off.

2. Take control of your explanatory style, that is, the way you interpret past events to yourself. Put a positive twist on things or "spin it" to your benefit, as they say in politics, by looking back and reinterpreting any seemingly negative situation and mentally downplaying or minimizing its significance. This reduces the effect the past has on your future.

3. Watch out for media programming, the constant suggestive influence from radio, television, newspaper, magazines, and billboards. It's estimated that the average American is exposed to more than 1,500 advertising messages each day. If you think like the masses think, you'll get what the masses get.

4. Never let anyone say anything to you or about you in your presence that you don't sincerely want to happen. Be alert whenever someone starts a sentence with the word "you" in daily conversations. Your interactions with others play a major role in what you believe to be true about yourself. Sometimes it's minor. Sometimes it's major. But everything counts! Be especially cognizant of old friends who continue to speak of you as the person you *used* to be, but no longer *want* to be.

5. In dealing with other people, particularly those you live or work with, never refer to someone or characterize someone in their presence as something you don't want them to be or you'll just be reinforcing their tendency to be that way. If you want somebody to be on time more often, then the very worst thing you can do is to shout at them or look them in the eye and say, "You're always late!" Avoid this temptation or you'll keep getting more of the same!

6. Whenever you catch yourself thinking something negative or self-defeating, say the word "cancel," "next," or "deflect," then say or think what you really want to believe. This technique interrupts and weakens limiting patterns of thought.

7. By always doing what you say, you strengthen your character and literally program yourself to create the reality dictated by your words. So resolve to keep every single agreement you make with yourself and your self-talk will become even more powerful. In other words, walk your talk.

8. Refuse to claim things or stake your possession to anything that you don't want in your lifestyle such as *my* cold, *my* headache, *my* bad back, *my* debt, or *my* price range. Instead, attach yourself mentally and verbally to what you *do* want such as peace of mind, happiness, prosperity, and perfect health.

9. No matter how common it may be, refuse to get cornered into conversations involving skepticism, cynicism, doubt, fear, worry or gossip. Self-talk is quite contagious. Don't let others contaminate your self-talk with their negativity. Only talk to yourself and others about things you want to happen.

10. Most people routinely say things to themselves or about themselves that they would never, ever say to a respected friend. Refuse to acknowledge or give air time to any thoughts that are in opposition to who you really want to be. Be a respected and nourishing friend to yourself.

11. Leave the past in the past. If it becomes necessary to discuss a habit, tendency, or quality that you'd rather not have, always talk about it as if it's long gone, as if it's history rather than a current, ongoing problem. Use the phrases "up until now," "in the past," or "I used to be" to frame any constructive self-criticism. Be careful not to pull the past into the future by making generalizations about prior behavior.

12. Choose the words of champions. Replace "I'll try to" with "I will." Replace "I didn't have time" with "I chose not to make time for that." Replace "It's not my fault" with "I accept responsibility." Replace "You make me upset" with "I feel upset when..." You always have the choice. You can be a helpless victim or you can be a powerful and impactful human being.

13. Watch out for others who transplant their past experiences to you, often lowering your expectations and, in effect, causing you to clinch up, preparing for the worst. This is particularly true concerning life's common experiences such as school exams, dating, marriage, pregnancy, raising children, finances, and getting older. Learn from others' experience, but always assume it's going to be a lot better for you than it was for them. Remember, what you expect with confidence tends to materialize. So, be alert to the sort of mass hypnotism that goes on in our society.

14. Every cell in your body "listens in" to your thinking and interprets each thought as a command. If you want to know what your self-talk was like three years ago, just look at yourself and your life today. What the mind harbors, the body expresses.

15. Putting into practice even just a few suggestions from this lesson will generate a visible and measurable improvement in your life. Don't worry about mistakes, tripping up a little or falling back. Shrug it off and stay focused on doing better tomorrow. Remember, it is at the *very moment* that you think your self-talk is not working that you need to use it the most. Fill up every spare moment with a thought of the person you want to be.

You Are Changing!

Finally, remember this: At this very moment you are changing! Nobody stays the same for any length of time. You are continually and constantly changing in the specific direction that your thoughts and goals lead you. You are what you are and where you are because of the dominating thoughts you have allowed to occupy your mind. Your surroundings are nothing more than the out-picturing of your thoughts. And there's only one thing in the world that you have complete and total control over and that is your thinking. If you don't deliberately and constructively give yourself positive directions, your mind and your body, like a vacuum, will continue to suck up and act upon instructions and directions from anywhere and everywhere. There's no argument. It's easier to do nothing and just take life as it comes to you. But you have a choice: You can be programmed by your fears and doubts, by envious peers and fair weather friends, by the flood of bad news and negative headlines, or you can chart your own course and let others follow. It's completely up to you. Do you now have the intensity of purpose, the tenacity, to discipline your mind to stay fixed on what you want and off of what you don't want? If you do, your mind will become magnetized with confidence and boldness. Using the tool of positive self-talk, you can eliminate negative thought patterns and replace them with positive beliefs and expectations. Using self-talk you can make the internal adjustments that must precede all external changes. You can discover much more out of life than most people ever look for. You are mentally tough! And I know you can do it!

Lesson 5
Assignments

1. *Make a list of what you would believe about yourself, your potential, and the world if you had already achieved your most important goal.*

2. *On separate notecards, neatly write at least 10 self-talk statements (affirmations) for each of your top five 3-year goals.*

3. *Read aloud the "15 Practical Insights" on pages 140-143.*

<u>Lesson 6</u>

Choose Positive Visualization

*Positive results follow
positive mental pictures.*

Discipline Your Mind

Sharpen Your Concentration Ability

Reinforce Commitment to Goals

Increase Desire

Build Productive Beliefs

Reduce Stress

Accelerate Your Progress

subconscious programming technique even more powerful than positive self-talk is positive visualization — mentally picturing events or outcomes in your mind's eye before they occur in physical reality. Visualization works based on the same principles as self-talk, but it is considerably more effective because it goes directly to the source. The "source" is the collection of subconscious mental pictures that occupy your mind. Self-talk influences and triggers the development of new mental images, whereas visualization imprints the new pictures directly. Self-talk and visualization complement each other. Visualization intensifies your self-talk and self-talk reinforces your visualization. Both techniques promote the accomplishment of your goals and should be used in tandem on a consistent basis.

It's important to note that visualization is a skill which can be learned and mastered. Everyone has the ability to visualize. As with every other skill, some find visualization naturally more easy, almost intuitive, while others must practice often to really experience the benefits. Just thinking of how many windows there are in your living room or thinking what it's like to bite into a lemon or the smell of freshly baked chocolate chip cookies demonstrates your ability to visualize. Visualization refers not just to visual images but also to hearing, touch, taste, smell, and self-generated emotional sensations. It has been said that the pictures you create in your head turn into the reality you hold in your hand. That's why it is crucial that you not allow the visualization process to be arbitrary and haphazard. The primary aim of this lesson is to help you make the shift from random, reactive visualizations to deliberate, proactive visualizations that support who you want to become and what you want to accomplish.

For the rest of this lesson, I will teach you exactly what visualization means, how it works, variations of visualization, and how to enhance your visualization powers so you maximize your performance in every area of life.

Your subconscious mind is responsible for your long-term success, failure, or mediocrity. It is responsible for generating and coordinating every element of your thinking, feeling, speaking, and acting. This is good news because you are responsible for the subconscious mind and whether it is programmed for success. Once again, you are in charge. You have yet another opportunity to take control of the direction of your life if, and this is a big "if," you are willing to be extraordinarily picky about which thoughts occupy your mind. While you cannot always control what you are exposed to and the thoughts these exposures stimulate, you can control what you choose to dwell upon. It is the thoughts you harbor most often that impact your life the most. It is the thoughts that "set up camp" in your mind which have the most influence, not those that merely drop in for a quick visit. Fortunately, your subconscious mind is not a master, but an ever-ready and willing servant. It will bring into your life whatever you sincerely and passionately ask it for. The subconscious isn't discriminating either. **Like fertile soil, your subconscious will accommodate whatever seeds you choose to plant.** It's just as happy to help you or hurt you. It is happy to bring you health or sickness and fatigue. It is just as happy to bring you abundance as it is lack. Your mind works on the instructions it is given. These instructions can come from its owner or they can come from whatever influences the owner exposes himself to on a regular basis. It is up to you to give your subconscious mind instructions that will produce a life and lifestyle that will make you happy.

An "instruction" can be defined as any continuously held conscious thought. It is not the infrequent mental pictures that exert tremendous influence, but the most dominant ones. **It is the images that are dwelled upon consciously and repeatedly that get absorbed like a sponge onto the mental software of the subconscious mind.** At this point the progress is made or the damage is done. Successful men and women train their minds to think about what they want to have happen in their lives. They think about the type of person

> *I visualized where I wanted to be, what kind of player I wanted to become. I knew exactly where I wanted to go, and I focused on getting there.*
> —Michael Jordan

they want to become. They think about their goals and dreams. They think about the principles and virtues they most admire. They think about the people they like and the situations they hope to experience. The unsuccessful or mediocre lack mental discipline. Their thoughts drift from the circumstances they hope to avoid to the people they dislike and the wide variety of injustices that seem to surround them. They're quick to dismiss themselves as being unlucky and even quicker to dismiss the successful as being extremely lucky. The mediocre bathe themselves in all the reasons why they can't have the life they really want and, lo and behold, they end up being right.

Your subconscious mind is incapable of distinguishing between an actual event and one that is only imagined. This God-given dynamic of the human brain allows you, through repeated visualizations, to convince your subconscious mind that a desired goal has already been accomplished. And once your mind believes something to be true, it automatically adjusts your thoughts, words, emotions, and behaviors to be consistent with that of your visualization. A visualization is a by-product of an electrical and chemical process within the brain. Because your visual images are composed of electromagnetic energy that consists of matter, they are, in effect, real. As a result, your mind and body interpret them as reality and respond to your visualizations as though they were actually happening. For example, during mental rehearsals of their events, Olympic athletes often experience physiological changes — increased heart rate, respiration, perspiration, or even involuntary muscle movements — as if they were participating in the real event. Best of all, according to Stanford neurosurgeon and psychologist, Dr. Karl Pribram, electromagnetically charged visual images produce a magnetic field that attracts back to the visualizer those things he vividly imagines and senses. This phenomenon enables you to attract into your life the very people, resources, and circumstances necessary to translate your goal into concrete reality.

Two Types of Visualization

You can visualize two primary aspects of a goal. One is the specific outcome itself. The other is the process or series of steps you must take to get there. It is important to practice both, but if you have to choose, practice outcome visualization because it is the realization of the actual goal that counts the most, not necessarily how you get there.

In outcome visualizations, you rehearse the achievement of your goal in rich sensory detail. You should focus on the exact moment that represents attainment of the goal. Outcome visualization keeps you excited and motivated, especially during the inevitable glitches, delays or temporary disappointments. The more your eye is on the goal, the more focused and determined you will be.

In process visualization, you mentally preview the necessary steps to accomplish your goal. World-class athletes invest the time not only to envision the desired end result, but also to clearly see how they want to get there. The more an athlete mentally practices, the better his performance becomes. The mind actually trains the body to perform

What If?

What if you visualized (100 times) pushing away a dessert after taking only one bite. Do you think you'd be more likely to do that in real circumstances?

What if you visualized (100 times) making your next presentation comfortably and in excellent fashion. Do you think that would have a positive impact on your results?

What if you visualized (100 times) the physical condition you hope to be in when you turn 60. Do you think that would have any effect on the lifestyle habits you choose today?

What if you visualized (100 times) rising easily and effortlessly at 5 a.m. feeling completely refreshed and rejuvenated. Do you believe that would improve your effectiveness in the morning?

just as it did in the mental rehearsal. Since the mind is the only place where you can practice perfectly, it behooves you to work out there often. The more you see yourself performing effectively, the more comfortable, confident, and relaxed you will feel in the actual event, and the better you will perform. This sense of familiarity breeds excellent results.

The Seven Components of Successful Visualization

Enhancing any of the seven components of effective visualization will expedite the physical manifestation of the visualized image.

1. Relaxation: How relaxed you are when you picture something you want to occur plays a major role in how fast the desired mental image becomes rooted in the subconscious. And it has to get rooted in the subconscious before it becomes a reality. Tension, anxiety, and worry tend to hamper concentration and block the formation and mental crystallization of your goals. Take the necessary time to get deeply relaxed. It is very important not to feel rushed or that there is something else more valuable that you should be doing.

2. Frequency: The more frequently you visualize a goal, the more that goal will tend to influence the way you think, talk, feel, and act. You will become more likely to engage in activities that move you toward your goal and progressively less inclined to do things that slow your progress. The benefits of every act of visualization accumulate like a giant snowball generating momentum for the accomplishment of your goal. The more committed you are to continually previewing your goals on your personal video screen, the more quickly you will see and experience tangible results.

3. Clarity: The more clear you are about any goal you hope to achieve, the more motivated and inspired you will be to accomplish it. Likewise, when you clearly and distinctly imagine the accomplishment of your goal, your enthusiasm, desire, and creativity soar. Imagine discussing with your spouse the characteristics and qualities of your future dream home. Imagine only discussing the size, style, location, number of bedrooms, and price. While that is a good start, imagine the difference in your excitement

Two Types of Visualization

Outcome

Focus on the exact moment that represents attainment of your goal.

Process

Mentally preview the steps or actions necessary to reach your goal.

and motivation to move in when you start considering the special features that appeal to you individually and as a couple. The neighborhood, the master bedroom design, the big closet in the garage, the ready finished hardwood floors, the automatic hot water dispenser, and the deck overlooking the garden are all important details that add life to your picture. Considering all the possibilities and envisioning how you will personalize the house into a home helps complete the mental equivalent.

Always remember to add as much detail to your visualization as possible. Make it graphic, colorful and vividly rich. It is the existence of small details that makes your mental pictures seem authentic. **The more skilled you become at precisely duplicating in your head what you want to see in your life, the more rapidly your goals will appear.** The inability to see the small, unique features in your visualization is a strong clue that you are not making the progress you are capable of making.

4. Duration: The longer you can hold a crisp, clear picture of your goal, the sooner and more likely it is to appear. Each time you visualize, attempt to hold the picture a little bit longer than the time before. Refuse to let fear, worry, distractions, or any other type of resistance cut short the length of each act of visualization or your commitment to stick with it. All forms of real and imagined resistance begin to dissolve the longer you hold a concrete mental image of the goal you desire. The more you practice visualization, the stronger your ability to concentrate becomes. With practice, you will be able to lock out all extraneous thoughts that weaken and dilute the focus of your mental movie.

5. Emotion: The more emotional intensity you can generate while picturing your goals, the faster new mental commands are accepted by your subconscious mind. When you visualize, really concentrate on manufacturing the precise feelings that would accompany the accomplishment

The 7 Components of Effective Visualization

of your goal. Then amplify, or even exaggerate, those feelings over and over until they are internalized. To produce positive, forceful emotional states, it's helpful to remind yourself of the many wonderful benefits you will receive when your goal is reached. **Mentally celebrate in advance by pretending your goal has already been accomplished.** Drench yourself in the feelings of satisfaction, gratitude, and inner peace just as you would if you actually reached your goal. Take in all the sensations of the experience you are imagining.

6. Perspective: This refers to the point of view you take while visualizing. The perspective from which your mental picture originates influences its overall strength, clarity, and intensity. As you visualize, if you are looking through your own eyes at the accomplishment of your goal, you are fully associated in your mind. This means you are the "player." You are seeing and sensing from the perspective of the participant. You are in the game and experience all the relevant sensations. This "associated" perspective supercharges your central nervous system with a sense of passion, excitement and exhilaration.

The other perspective is called "dissociation." When your visualization is dissociated, you are watching yourself through the eyes of a spectator, rather than through your own eyes. It's like watching yourself in a home movie. Imagine sitting at a traffic light and looking over at the car next to you and noticing that it is you. This is the dissociated point of view. While most people have a natural tendency to visualize as associated or dissociated, either perspective can be mastered with patience and practice.

The dissociated perspective is helpful for minimizing the emotional impact of any event, just as a spectator of a World Series game doesn't experience the same intensity of emotions as the players, though they can be very involved.

The associated perspective should be used when you want to boost the excitement, motivation, and energy of your mental image by being in the game, seeing it through your own eyes.

7. Scripting: It is crucial to have a written script that details every aspect of your visualization. Your script need not be long, but it should contain all the key aspects of the imagined event with as many details as possible. Again, it is the details that bring authenticity to your imagination. **Describing your visualization in writing will force you to crystallize your thinking.** If there are any gaps in your mental picture, they will become apparent as you try to translate your visual story into the written word. I have found with my clients that a visualization script often provides the tangible tool that encourages consistent use of an otherwise nebulous, intangible exercise. Very few people are disciplined enough to create and implement a visual-

The Perspective
While Visualizing

The Player
*You are **in** the game and experience all the relevant sensations.*

Either perspective can be mastered with patience and practice.

The Spectator
Like watching yourself in a home movie.

ization exercise regularly without some sort of prompter. The presence of the script tends to make you much more inclined to practice. And the more you practice visualization, the better you get. A good, reasonable script will probably be about one to one-and-a-half typed, double-spaced pages. Most importantly, make sure you include all essential details without mixing in any extraneous words or phrases.

Here are some ideas to help you pull your visualization script together. First, state your specific goal in the form of an affirmation.

- Why is reaching this goal important to you? What are the benefits? Include specific and non-specific benefits as well as tangible and intangible benefits.

- Imagine the exact moment that you accomplished this goal or fulfilled your dream. What event would most represent this accomplishment?

- If this were happening right now, how would you feel? Step into that moment. Pretend you are there right now. What emotions would be most dominant?

- What do you see around you that is evidence of your accomplishment?

- What are you doing?

- Sounds. What do you hear? Clapping, laughter, music, chatter, ocean waves, etc.

- Sense of smell. What scents stand out? Chocolate chip cookies, new car, salty air, perfume, garlic, flowers, cologne, other unique scents.

> *In 1990 actor and comedian Jim Carrey wrote himself a check for 10 million dollars. On the check he wrote for "acting services rendered" and post-dated it Thanksgiving 1995. He carried the check in his wallet, looking at it daily until he signed a 10 million dollar contract to star in The Mask 2 almost a year ahead of his target date.*

- Touch. What are you holding, sitting on or leaning against? Handshakes, pats, clothing, furniture, etc.

- Taste. What are you tasting? Champagne, shrimp cocktail, brownies, chocolate mint ice-cream, mouthwash, Gatorade, etc.

- What words or phrases capture this experience?

- Which of your values are most reflected by what you see?

Visual Triggers

In addition to mentally rehearsing your goals, it is also effective to surround yourself with visual representations of your goals or ideal lifestyle. Having these visual reminders in your environment is an effortless way to stay focused and motivated. Constantly be on the lookout for photographs, quotes, headlines, sketches, and other items that remind you of your goals. The reminders do not have to be exactly the same as what you are after. They just need to symbolize your goals and aspirations. Of course, if you can

* To order *The Secret Place* Compact Disc which guides you through several deep relaxation and visualization exercises, please call 1-800-643-9770 or visit our Web site at www.1percentclub.com

find exact pictures, those work best. For example, if your goal is to be lean and muscular by weighing your ideal weight of 175 pounds, find a picture of yourself when you were lean and put it on the refrigerator door. If you cannot find the right picture of yourself, simply cut out a picture from a fitness magazine of someone who has the "look" you're shooting for. Keep the picture anywhere you will see it often. In a weight loss situation, the refrigerator tends to work best. One of my clients took a slightly different approach to improving her health by placing photos of healthy gourmet meals on her refrigerator.

Here are some other examples:

If your goal is to earn $100,000 by December 31, your visualization device might be a picture of a large stack of $100 dollar bills or it might be the numbers $100,000 spelled out and colored in or it might simply be a photograph of something you will buy when you earn the money.

If your goal is to travel to Fiji, then your visualization trigger would likely be pictures of Fiji from a travel brochure or magazine along with the dates you plan to be there.

If your goal is to read the Bible from cover to cover in the next three years, your visualization device might be a Polaroid of yourself sitting in your study with your Bible and a clock in the background showing 5 a.m. And also maybe a cup of hot coffee.

Try a Goal Map!

A Goal Map is a large visual reminder of a goal or group of goals you want to accomplish. To create your goal map, attach pictures, photos, sketches, headlines or other visual stimulators of the goal you are pursuing to a poster or bulletin board. In the center of the board, using several different colors of ink, print your goal in bold, block letters. Then paste or pin your picture around the statement of your goal. Magazines, brochures, catalogs, and newspapers are good sources to get you started. Some goal maps I've seen are very neat and logically organized, while others are more

When my wife, Kristin, decided she was ready to be a mother (about 6 months before we officially began trying to conceive) she found a newspaper photograph of a man that closely resembled me (although not quite as handsome!) holding and playing with a beautiful baby. Kristin pinned the picture up on a mini-bulletin board in our shared walk-in closet. Day after day, with barely any effort or intention, we both got a glimpse of the picture. It was as if we were looking into a crystal ball. Did it work? Well, we both, of course, had to do our part, but conception did occur within the first month! I still show this photograph to many of my clients. Stay tuned....My wife just put up another picture.

like a collage. Experiment and see which approach works best for you. You may want to intersperse affirmations or quotations with your pictures on the goal map as well. I've used some variation of a goal map for years, and at the very least it has kept me more motivated, inspired and enthusiastic. At one point, I had a separate goal map (bulletin board) for each area of my life hung up on the walls of my exercise room. Visualizing and exercising is a wonderful combination. By the way, each of the goals represented on the goal maps has now been accomplished.

If you don't have much room to devote to your goal maps, then try hanging it up on the back of a closet door or sliding it under your bed and pulling it out every night for review before you go to sleep. **By flooding your mind with a constant stream of success images, you displace old self-defeating doubts, fears, and insecurities.**

> *I've encouraged a number of my clients to create and regularly review ideal future financial statements that represent where they want to be financially 9, 18, and 36 years down the road. This is particularly easy with the money management software packages available today. Try putting together your ideal Net Worth statement for 9 or 18 years from now! Look at them often.*

Create a Future Scrapbook

A variation of the goal map is a "future scrapbook." It serves the same purpose and can be more private and convenient. Make your "future scrapbook" a preview of your life's coming attractions. Fill it out with pictures, quotations, affirmations, and any mementos that symbolize the course you want your life to take. It should be the visual story of your life. To get started, simply collect pictures and other items as you would for a goal map and paste them to sheets of paper or card stock. Then insert them into or laminate them and put inside a 3-ring binder. A photo album could also serve the same purpose. There is virtually no limit on the different approaches you could take in putting together a "future scrapbook"! Just be creative and review often, especially right before bedtime and immediately upon arising in the morning.

The more visual cues you can place around you, the more often you'll be triggered to think about your goals, and the less you'll be tempted to think about what you *don't want*. Also, the very act of searching for the appropriate pictures and reminders of success will stimulate your reticular activating system and help you be more alert to the people and resources necessary to transform your dreams into realities.

Lesson 6
Assignments

1. Complete a visualization script for one of your top five 3-year goals.

2. Invest 10 to 15 minutes a day re-reading the script and imagining that your goal is already a reality.

3. Collect visual reminders (pictures, quotes, sketches, etc.) for each of your top 5 goals and place them where you will effortlessly see them daily.

Lesson 7

Choose a High-Energy Lifestyle

Neglect is a silent killer.

Make health-producing choices

Develop a positive mental attitude

Control stress

Exercise intelligently

Eat for energy

Sleep for success

Relax and rejuvenate

oundless energy is not an accident. Individuals who experience a continuous, revitalizing flow of energy make different choices than those who consistently operate from an energy deficit. You can increase your return on energy and your return on life by becoming highly sensitive to the choices you make regarding your lifestyle. Remember, your level of energy equals your level of health. If you are short on energy, you are short on life. Every area of your life will be compromised by a depleted supply of energy. More than any other factor, a lack of energy will cause you to underachieve and under perform. As Vince Lombardi said, "Fatigue does make cowards of us all." When you are run-down, drained, or otherwise out of balance, the quality of your choices is negatively influenced. Your choices become more oriented around the short term. You think more about what is expedient than what is in your long-term best interests. You act defensively and reactively.

Abundant levels of energy are the indispensable prerequisite for individual achievement, success, and peace of mind.

Fortunately, becoming a high-energy, high-output human being need not be a gamble. The causes of vigorous energy have been thoroughly researched and well documented. Superior levels of energy and vitality are the natural consequence of putting into place the causes of high energy outlined in the rest of this lesson.

7 Keys to a High-Energy Lifestyle

1. Write down a goal for how long you want to live healthfully and productively.

This should be a goal to live to at least the age of 80. Once you have set this goal you begin to organize your lifestyle around health habits that are consistent with living productively and healthfully to age 80 or older. The best way to do this is to take a sheet of paper and draw a line down the center. On the left side, write down everything you can do that will help you live to at least age 80. On the right hand side, write down all the negative habits or activities you may be tempted to engage in that would hurt your chance of reaching 80. Once completed, begin to eliminate, one by one, all the negative health habits and begin introducing to your life, or reinforcing, the positive health habits.

2. Develop a positive mental attitude.

Your attitude is the habitual way you think. Over the long haul, the quality of your life will be determined by the quality of your attitude. A high-energy lifestyle requires that you choose a positive mental attitude. A positive mental attitude is not something that happens to you. It is a deliberate choice which ultimately becomes a habit.

> **Everything can be taken away from a man but one thing: the last of the human freedoms — to choose one's attitude in any given set of circumstances, to choose one's own way.**
> **— Victor E. Frankl**

The more positive you are, the more energy you will have. **You become positive by deciding in advance that you will always choose the most resourceful response to any given set of circumstances.** This means that even if you are justified to do otherwise, you will always take the high road, choosing to act in a manner consistent with the goals you want to reach and the person you want to become.

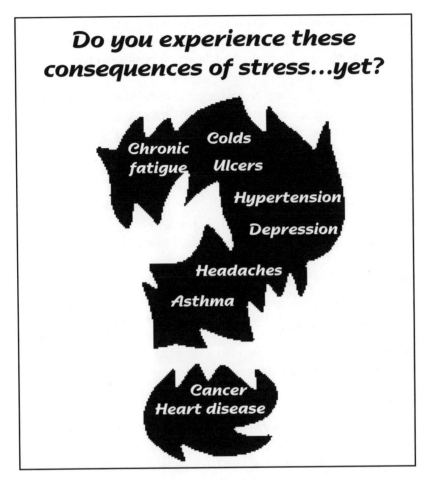

Do you experience these consequences of stress...yet?

Chronic fatigue
Colds
Ulcers
Hypertension
Depression
Headaches
Asthma
Cancer
Heart disease

3. Control stress.

We experience negative stress when we feel out of control of the sequence of events in our lives. It's like being in a fast moving car without a steering wheel. We experience stress when we live inconsistently with what we have identified as most important to us. Most of all, **we experience stress when we recognize that we are living far beneath our potential.**

The inability to deal effectively with stress has been linked to cancer, asthma, headaches, depression, cardiovascular disease, common cold, ulcers, hypertension, chronic fatigue, and immune system suppression, to name but a few. Mounting research indicates nearly 80 percent of all illness can be linked at least partially to psychological stress.

Stress is an extremely subjective condition. What causes some to get stressed out causes others to get excited and creative. Some people thrive on change while others will avoid change and the stress that goes with it at all costs. For some it is the big things that cause stress while for others it is the accumulation of little things.

Ask yourself this question: "Have I ever been stressed out without thinking stressful thoughts?"

I can guarantee you have not. It would be impossible. The bottom line on stress is this: It is the way in which you interpret your circumstances that triggers a stress response. It is the meaning you place on a certain event that makes it stressful, not the event itself. Start paying closer attention to the habitual way you describe mistakes and unpleasant situations to yourself and others. Finding a positive angle on a negative situation goes a long way to minimizing stress. The very act of searching for something good redirects your attention and keeps you in a productive, resourceful state. Remember, **it is the way you think about something that makes it stressful**. Stress doesn't really exist except to the degree to which you allow it. Your thoughts create emotions which in turn mold your thinking. Your thoughts, via neurochemicals, electrical charges and trillions of special receptors, influence every cell in your body. This is how conditions on the outside, negatively interpreted, produce harmful physiological changes on the inside.

Unless you deliberately develop an effective, perpetual stress management system, you will undercut your performance and face greater risk of disease.

Here are some tips to get you started:

• Follow all the other keys to a high-energy lifestyle outlined in this lesson.

> *Some things are within our control, and some things are not. It is only after you have faced up to this fundamental rule and learned to distinguish between what you can and can't control that inner tranquillity and outer effectiveness become possible.*
>
> *— Epictetus*

• Practice mental discipline. Choose what you think about (See Lesson 5).

• Make a personal stress inventory. Write down all the "stressors" in your life right now and one step you could take to alleviate them. Accepting that a difficult situation is real and clearly identifying or revealing the enemy is an important step. Proper diagnosis is half the cure.

• Simplify your life. Eliminate and concentrate. Focus on the vital few things that contribute the most to your overall life satisfaction. Taking on too much or spreading yourself too thin inevitably leads to a sense of overburden.

4. Combine aerobic, strength and flexibility exercises.

If you want maximum levels of energy, then it only makes sense that you take the responsibility for becoming a mini-expert on exercise and fitness. Subscribe to the most credible fitness and exercise magazines and build your own library full of the latest books, videos, and other resources related to energy and fitness.

The most important component of intelligent exercise is aerobic exercise. Aerobics or cardiovascular endurance refers to the sustained ability of the heart, lungs, and blood to perform optimally. Through consistent aerobic conditioning, oxygen uptake, transport, and utilization are improved. This means your heart and lungs will be stronger and more effective at performing their functions. Proper aerobic exercise causes your body to burn fat, while anaerobic exercise causes the body to burn glycogen and store fat. Many people unknowingly exercise anaerobically when they intended to exercise aerobically. This results in, among other things, a frustrating retention of fat. It is the intensity of your exercise that makes it anaerobic or aerobic.

Here are just a few of the benefits of consistent and proper aerobic exercise:
- improves quality of sleep
- relieves stress and anxiety
- burns excess fat
- suppresses appetite
- enhances attitude/mood
- stabilizes chemical balance
- brightens self-esteem

Each of the above benefits either directly or indirectly leads to high levels of both mental and physical energy.

Here are some tips for maximizing the quality of your aerobic workouts:

- Work out aerobically three to six times a week for at least 30 minutes.

- Use the "talk test" to stay within your target heart rate and gain the maximum fat burning benefits. Your exercise intensity should allow you to work out steadily while still being able to talk without gasping for breath.

- Use a calm, steady, enjoyable pace. Correct aerobic intensity is strenuous but still pleasurable.

- Instead of stretching your cold muscles before exercising, spend three to five minutes doing light, easy motions that mimic your sport or aerobic activity to warm them up.

- Also take about five minutes to gradually cool down after your workout. Never stop exercising suddenly. Following your workout, keep moving at a progressively slower and slower pace. This cool down period allows your heart

Benefits of Consistent Aerobic Exercise

1. Improves sleep

2. Relieves stress

3. Burns fat

4. Suppresses appetite

5. Enhances attitude

6. Stabilizes chemical balance

7. Fortifies immune system

8. Heightens self-esteem

rate and body systems to safely return to their pre-exercise state.

• Vary your aerobic routine throughout the week, or at least week to week. Alternating between several different aerobic activities develops a more balanced state of fitness and prevents boredom, which ultimately leads to the sofa.

• Drink lots of water before, during and after aerobic exercise. Pure water is best and research indicates that ice cold water enters the digestive track faster and activates the metabolism better than room temperature water. Plan ahead so that ample water is convenient and accessible.

• Whenever possible, blend your aerobic workout with a mental workout by listening to relaxing and inspirational music, listening to self-development tapes or visualizing your goal achievement. Try to think healthy, energetic and

empowering thoughts as this will energize you and complement your physical workout. As tempting as it may be,
avoid the news and newspapers as you exercise. **Make your
workouts completely positive experiences.**

The next component of intelligent exercise is strength
training. Proper strength training improves muscle tone,
balance, coordination and, of course, overall vibrancy. Including strength, or progressive resistance training in your
workout regimen will help you burn extra fat, resist fatigue, and avoid nagging injuries in addition to looking
and feeling better.

Muscle is the primary energy burner in your body so
the more toned you are, the more excess body fat you will
burn in a 24-hour period. With less fat, you will be more
energetic. And with more strength, you will develop more
endurance for work and everyday tasks, leaving you with
additional energy for other enjoyable projects and activities.

Flexibility is the most lonely component of intelligent
exercise as it is the most often left out. Proper stretching
energizes the body and the mind. As my Choi Kwang Do
instructor repeatedly told me, a flexible body equals a flexible mind. Done properly, stretching reduces tension, promotes circulation, improves posture and balance, increases
range of motion, and helps prevent injuries. In addition, it
just feels invigorating. After stretching, you'll want to be
more active and productive. Here are some guidelines for
effective stretching:

• Remember that before stretching you should do very
light movement that mimics your sport or exercise activity. This increases blood flow to your muscles and makes
them more supple, limber, and prepared for stretching.

• Stay relaxed throughout all stretching exercises. This
requires a deliberate effort at first. Repeatedly tell yourself
that you are relaxed, flexible, and resilient.

• Slowly move in and out of each stretch. Avoid bounc-
ing.

7 Steps to
High-Energy Nutrition

1. Plan your meals.

2. Eat low-fat to very low-fat foods.

3. Eat frequent small meals and light snacks.

4. Work in five or more servings of fresh fruit and vegetables.

5. Limit the white poisons: sugar, salt, bleached flour.

6. Drink lots of water.

7. Supplement your diet with an all-natural, high-quality vitamin and mineral formula.

• Breathe slowly, deeply and continuously. Holding your breath promotes tenseness.

• Go at your own pace. Enjoy and don't rush.

5. Eat for energy.

The foods you choose to eat throughout the day exert a powerful impact on your level of energy. Just a few small changes in your diet can cause you to experience a surge of mental and physical vitality. Here are seven steps to high-energy nutrition:

1. Take the time to plan your meals. Planned meals are much more likely to include smart nutritional choices that promote energy, health and well being. Most Americans find themselves in such a constant rush that what they eat is based on convenience and expediency rather than nutrition. **Planning meals puts you back in control.** It is also likely to save you time and money at the grocery store and help you avoid impulse buys.

2. Eat low fat to very low fat foods. Current recommendations are that total fat intake be less than 30 percent of calories. For peak performing energy, a 20 percent total fat goal is more appropriate. The easiest way to stay away from fat is to become a vegetarian or semi-vegetarian by eliminating or drastically reducing your intake of animal and dairy products. Be alert to the subtle fats found in sauces, gravies, dressing, and oils used in the cooking process, particularly when dining out.

3. Eat frequent small meals and very light snacks. Large meals overburden your digestive system and interfere with absorption of nutrients. Big meals, especially those high in fat or refined foods, lead to post-meal lethargy and low performance. If you are really serious about generating more energy, make your breakfast the biggest and most nutritionally sound meal of the day. Your body and brain will function better and your energy level will stay more consistent into the evening when you enjoy breakfast within 90 minutes of rising. Eating a healthy breakfast also jump-starts your metabolism and decreases the likelihood of binge eating later in the day. High carbohydrate, moderate protein, low fat breakfasts work best. Lunch should be moderate to light and dinner should be the lightest meal of the day. Most Americans do the reverse, which makes little sense from a physiological or performance standpoint. Experiment with a light, low fat midmorning and mid-afternoon snack. This will boost mental performance and physical endurance and curb overeating at dinner time. If you eat an early supper, a late night, extremely high carbohydrate snack will tend to improve the quality of your sleep.

7 Keys to High Energy

1. *Set a goal for how long you want to live.*

2. *Maintain a positive attitude.*

3. *Control stress.*

4. *Excercise intelligently.*

5. *Eat for energy.*

6. *Sleep for success.*

7. *Take time for rejuvenation.*

4. Work in five or more servings of fresh fruits and vegetables throughout your small meals and snacks during the day. Fruits and vegetables are naturally high in vitamins, minerals, fiber, antioxidants, and the recently discovered phytochemicals which protect the body from cell damage. Make fruits and vegetables the main course and relegate meats, pastas, and dairy products to the role of side dish. Go for the most colorful combinations of fruits and vegetables as this indicates richer nutrient content.

5. Limit sugar, salt and refined white flour! Collectively, these are referred to as the three white poisons because they offer little if any nutritional value and are known to contribute to a host of health problems. There is no need for added sugar in the body, yet the average American consumes nearly 200 pounds of additional sugar every year in the form of desserts, breakfast pastries, soft drinks, candy, jams, syrups, and alcohol, just to name a few. In addition to hampering the fat-burning process, simple sugars — often disguised as corn syrup, maltose, dextrose, dextrin, honey, or molasses — reduce your appetite for high nutrition foods and leave you feeling even more tired and sluggish after the initial pick-me-up wears off.

As with simple sugars, the human body needs little or no additional salt, yet many products on supermarket shelves have salt as a primary ingredient because of its preservative value. Many people also pour excessive amounts of salt on their food even before tasting it. By relying only on the natural salts found in your food, you'll start to enjoy a wider range of flavors that were previously neutralized with excessive salt. In addition, you'll maintain a healthy balance of sodium to potassium, which helps prevent cancer, heart disease, high blood pressure, and strokes.

Bleached or refined white flour, the third white poison, has been stripped of virtually all vitamin content and just about all fiber. It is, in effect, nutritionally dead. All white flour products, white rice, pasta, and crackers should be replaced with whole-grain pasta, breads, muffins, cereals, crackers, and brown rice. Though many white products claim to be enriched with vitamins, just remind yourself of what made them white.

6. Drink lots of water! The human body is composed of two-thirds water. Water is an essential nutrient involved in every function of the body. It helps transport nutrients and waste products in and out of cells. It's required for all digestive, absorption, circulatory, and excretory functions, as well as for the utilization of the water-soluble vitamins. It is also necessary for the maintenance of proper body temperature. Additionally, water suppresses the appetite naturally and helps the body eliminate stored fat. Often, thirst is mistaken for hunger and an unnecessary intake of calories is the result. When you feel hungry, but shouldn't be, first try drinking several cold glasses of water rapidly then waiting ten minutes or so, and often the food craving will pass. Quickly drinking several large cups of ice-cold water is also a terrific energy booster. Try it and see. By drinking at least eight to ten 8-ounce glasses of water every day, you can ensure that your body has what it needs to maintain peak health and vibrant energy.

7. Supplement your diet with an all natural, high quality multiple vitamin and mineral formula. Even if you eat a well-balanced diet, manage stress well, and exercise regularly, it is still a good idea to protect yourself with the "nutritional insurance" provided by a broad-spectrum vitamin, mineral, and antioxidant supplement. Be sure to choose supplements with expiration dates on the bottle to ensure maximum freshness. I'm a strong believer in natural food supplements and have been using a synergistic combination for many years. I encourage you to learn all you can about vitamins and supplementation, and begin working them into your overall high-energy fitness strategy.

6. Sleep for success.

This means you must consistently experience deep, rejuvenating sleep. Sufficient, refreshing sleep is essential to a high-energy lifestyle. Your body needs sleep to repair itself and function properly. As you sleep, you dream, allowing your subconscious to sort through unresolved psychological and emotional issues, brain waves slow down, blood pressure falls, muscles relax, the immune system is boosted, damaged tissues and cells are repaired, and the pituitary gland produces more hormones. Without sufficient sleep, the body is more likely to break down.

How much sleep you need depends on your unique make up as well as the other lifestyle choices you make. Research indicates that individuals who effectively deal with stress and negative emotions need less sleep time than those who are stressed out or worry chronically. Some people function best with only five to six hours of sleep while others may need as much as ten hours. On average the most effective rest tends to come from seven to eight hours of sleep. Improving the quality of your sleep can usually reduce the quantity of sleep needed.

Sleeping poorly night after night, or partial sleep deprivation, is a major cause of chronically low energy. Here are seven tips for achieving optimum sleep:

1. Arise at the same time every day. Don't "sleep in" on the weekends, at least not more than an hour. It confuses your body's biological clock. Oversleeping reduces alertness and energy in much the same way as jet lag. You reduce the amount of time you're awake making it tougher to fall asleep the next night.

2. Eat for deep sleep. Avoid caffeine products four to five hours prior to sleep. Also, drink alcohol not less than three to four hours prior to bedtime. While alcohol makes some people drowsy immediately afterward, it actually interferes with normal brain wave patterns of sleep pre-

7 Tips for Better Sleep

1. *Arise at the same time every day.*

2. *Eat for deep sleep.*

3. *Reserve the bedroom for sleep and sexual relations.*

4. *Develop a calming bedtime routine.*

5. *Make tomorrow's "to-do" list early.*

6. *Hide the clock!*

7. *Set the thermostat.*

venting deep, revitalizing sleep. Always eat a light evening meal. This will prevent too much energy from being used up for digestion while you're trying to get deep sleep. If you eat an early dinner, consider a very small nighttime snack that is low fat, low protein and high carbohydrate. This type of snack encourages a smoother transition into deep sleep while preventing a drop in blood sugar during the night that will disturb your sleep.

3. Reserve the bedroom for only sleep and sexual relations with your spouse. Your bedroom should be a comfortable, ultra-relaxing haven designed for peacefully letting go of the day. Avoid intense discussions, brainstorming, snacking, TV watching, financial planning and budgeting, and all work when you're in your bedroom. These types of activities promote excitement or agitation and work against a good night's sleep. When you only allow two activities in your bedroom, you condition yourself for successful sleep.

4. Develop a calming bedtime routine. You must have a workable system in place that helps you unwind and let go of the day. Applying certain relaxation techniques, listening to classical music or nature sounds, as well as prayer, affirmations, or inspirational readings all contribute to optimal sleep. Research also indicates that a hot bath or shower or moderate exercise within three hours of bedtime can significantly deepen sleep.

5. Put together your "to do" list before entering your bedroom, preferably several hours before going to bed or while still at work. Nothing encourages insomnia more than waiting until the morning to write down all that needs to be done. If ideas do come to you after the lights are out, then go ahead and unload them onto your list or into a recorder. Even if you're able to fall asleep, it only weakens your sleep to try to remember all that needs to be done the next day.

6. Hide the clock! Put your alarm clock where it can be heard but not seen. Sleep difficulty is only exacerbated by having a clock to look at, reinforcing how late it is. No one sleeps well under time pressure. Also, avoid getting jolted awake with a blaring alarm. How you awaken and what you do in those first few minutes sets the energy and performance tone of the rest of the day. Experiment with a positive music or affirmation alarm with the volume set just loud enough to notice it. Decide at night what you want your first thought of the next day to be. Make it an inspiring thought and repeat it to yourself as you drift to sleep. You'll be amazed as this thought races to your consciousness upon awakening. Remember, you're in charge. Don't leave it to chance.

7. Identify your most comfortable sleeping temperature. Sixty-five to 70 degrees tends to work best for most people. Invest in a firm, supporting mattress and arrange for a very dark, quiet bedroom. Even dim light and slight noise can damage the quality of your sleep even if you never wake up completely. Sleeping on your side, in the semi-fetal position with a supportive neck pillow tends to reduce tossing and turning.

7. Rest and rejuvenation.

In addition to proper sleep, it is crucial that you consciously schedule ample time to revitalize your mind. Optimum creativity and productivity requires mental rest. This means your brain, like your body, needs sufficient rest and renewal to operate at its peak. Unless you balance periods of intense mental work with periods of "doing nothing," or recovery, you are likely to experience chronic mental fatigue. Chronic mental fatigue begins with a feeling that you're not getting enough accomplished. This usually coincides with periods of high stress or mental and physical exhaustion. In order to compensate for the lack of accomplishment, you put in more time and push yourself even harder. This just makes you even more tired and ineffective, which leads to putting in even more hours and so on.

The quantity and, especially, the quality of your creative projects drops as your focus and judgment fade. The belief that you are actually crunching out good work is just an illusion. In addition, mounting fatigue and a tense, over-tired state tends to spill over into your family life generating more impatience and irritability. No skill is as valuable to your overall creativity, vitality and well-being as learning to disengage yourself from the compulsion toward constant busyness. Here are seven tips for letting go and replenishing your mental energy:

1. Take frequent five-minute stress breaks during the day to redirect your thinking to something fun and undemanding. Unplugging from the day's current of activity for just several minutes at a time will be surprisingly invigorating. Here are some ideas:

- Visualize a vacation.
- Review Bible verses.
- Think about your childhood.
- Flip through a catalog or photo album.

2. Take at least one 24-hour period a week where you do no mental or work-related activity. Research indicates this is more effective than working straight through.

3. Take a four-day vacation every 90 days. The point is to completely shut off your mental gears and refrain from doing any work.

4. Take at least two weeks of vacation each year where, again, there is no work or mentally demanding activity. Even if you really, really love what you do, it is simply not possible to relax and work. Just dabbling into light work on a vacation defeats the rejuvenating process. Whenever possible, go ahead and take the two weeks consecutively. If you have been driving yourself aggressively, it may take about a week to just unwind. The second week is most therapeutic.

5. Declutter your home, car and office. The presence of stuff scattered throughout your environment adds to

7 Tips for Replenishing Mental Energy

1. Take frequent 5-minute stress breaks.

2. Don't work for one day every week.

3. Take a 4-day vacation every quarter.

4. Take two weeks of vacation annually.

5. Declutter your home, car, office.

6. Get a massage.

7. Recultivate simple pleasures.

stress levels and a sense of overwhelm. Straightening up your environment alone can improve your sense of control and enthusiasm for life. Developing a systematic process of simplifying and streamlining can be refreshing and energizing.

6. Massage releases pent-up tensions and benefits the mind, body, and emotions. In addition to seeing a professional massage therapist, learn self-massage techniques so that massage can become a weekly habit. An hour is wonderful, but ten to fifteen minutes gets the job done.

7. Re-cultivate the simple pleasures of life: music, stars, sunset, poetry, garden, photos, home movies, journal (no TV).

Lesson 7
<u>*Assignments*</u>

1. Set a goal for how long you want to live healthfully and productively (your age and the year).

2. Make a list of all the lifestyle choices consistent with living productively and healthfully until the age you set for a goal in question 1.

3. Make a list of all the choices that are **not** consistent with living to your life span goal.

4. Write on a notecard the following self-talk statement: "My daily choices create my perfect health." Tape this notecard to your bathroom mirror!

<u>Afterword</u>

The Gold Medal Tax

_In America, we have the freedom
to succeed **and** the freedom to fail._

The pursuit of happiness

The politics of mediocrity

In the name of fairness

Robin Hood tactics

Something for nothing

Winning elections

or America to develop its full potential as a country, it must promote and encourage the individual success of its citizens. As Americans, we have the right to the pursuit of happiness, not the right to happiness itself. We have the right to equal opportunity, but not the right to equal results. We have the freedom to succeed and the freedom to fail. We have the right to make the choices in our lives we believe will make us happy. If we make wise choices, then we have the right to enjoy the fruits or effects of those choices. If we end up making the wrong choices, then we must naturally suffer the negative consequences. Fortunately, we then have the right to learn from our mistakes and make better choices in the future. We have the option of paying a bigger price and of earning a bigger reward. We have the right to plan more, read more, learn more, work more, practice more, risk more and become more than the person next to us. This means we also have the right to be better and achieve better results. We can exercise the equal opportunity to become unequal, or we can choose to be average.

Nothing is quite so damaging to the future of America as the proliferation of resentment and envy toward the minority of peak performing men and women who are frequently and collectively referred to by the media as "the rich." This negative attitude toward the financially successful is manifested in campaign slogans promising to "soak the rich" and "let's make the wealthy pay their fair share." There is no politician quite so cowardly as the one who seeks to gain personal power and position by dividing Americans by economic class. I call this type of class warfare, "The Politics of Mediocrity," and it is nothing less than poison to the American spirit. America was founded on the principles of self-reliance, limited government, private property, individual initiative, hard work, and daring. Individualism has made America the great country it is today. Consider the American lifestyle today without the likes of IBM, Microsoft, Federal Express, McDonald's, Ford, Home Depot, and Kodak.....all companies founded by exceptional individuals and all of which add tremendous value to our lives.

Promising to punish, through higher taxes, those who've already excelled financially and succeeded, as many Americans would love to do, sends a mediocre message to the rest of the population. It is like taxing a gold medal winner in the Olympics. Imagine, whoever wins the gold must have his medal melted down and redistributed to those who did not even place in the race. Isn't that a silly idea? Winning a gold medal or World Series ring will get you a trip to the White House, but winning your personal financial game will only get you a trip to your CPA. Being the best in athletics is admirable, but succeeding financially is politically incorrect or even sinister. Resenting the successful few has, in many respects, replaced baseball as the national pastime.

In the Name of Fairness

During the national crises created by World War I and World War II, the American people began to allow more and more government involvement in the economy through taxation and regulation. As American prosperity soared, many began to believe it was only fair for the government to take some away from those who were doing well and pass it along to those who were not doing quite so well. Many economists and academics began to embrace the socialistic concept of controlling the means of production as well as the distribution of goods produced. The idea of redistribution of America's wealth became a popular political strategy. Politicians would be in charge of taking from those who produced more and giving to those who produced less. Since the percentage of those who do really well (the top producers) tends to be quite small, it's fairly easy to gain mass support for taxing them. In other words, if you take from Peter and give to Paul, you will always have the vote of Paul, and Paul represents the majority of votes.

This Robin Hood tactic of penalizing the successful and re-appropriating their assets would never even get off the ground in America unless it were fueled by the natural human tendency to try to get *something for nothing*. This is an all too common delusion which is always shattered in the long run. You will only succeed financially and otherwise to the degree that you are able to resist the something-for-nothing urge that is so pervasive in our society. All lasting success comes from putting in far more than you plan to take out. **When individuals, via governmental interference, consume without producing, then others must produce without consuming.** Make a promise to yourself that you will expect rewards only *after* you create authentic value for others. Decide to consume only after first producing. These decisions will boost your self-esteem and your potential for great success.

Remember, when you punish the achievers, you hurt everyone else as an unintended and indirect consequence. Abraham Lincoln said, "You cannot help the poor by tearing down the rich. You cannot help the wage earner by hurting the wage payer." For a society to prosper, it must never forget *who* creates the jobs.

The creative minority who do are the envy of the masses who stand by and just watch. Those who promote the idea of assessing a punitive tax on the super productive minority seem to forget the lessons of history. You can look around the globe and see the destructive consequences of societies like the Soviet Union who, in the name of fairness and equality, tried to disallow success. These societies starved themselves from the ideas, services, products and jobs triggered by the so-called rich. As a result, they were unable to thrive and they eventually collapsed. While the strategy of class envy succeeds in winning elections from time to time, it never really helps the intended beneficiaries (unless the beneficiary is the politician) and, in the long run, hurts America by eroding and undermining the principles upon which it was built.

To argue against self-reliance, personal initiative and individual success is to take the easy route — the road most traveled.

Become a member of the Magnificent Minority. Accept that you are totally responsible for your success. Not the government, not your boss, not your parents, and not society. Only you. No one is coming to the rescue! Only you have the power to make the choices that will accumulate into the fruits of an exciting, successful, and satisfying life. Remember, the pursuit and attainment of success and happiness is completely up to you. Choose to take the initiative and you'll find opportunities you never imagined existed.

Appendix

What is The 1% Club®?

My Every Desire — Thought Stimulators

A Legendary Achiever

Free Self-Talk Cards

What is The 1% Club®?

The 1% Club® is a three-year life management program designed specifically to support the needs and challenges of the high-income individual.

Most 1% Club members are either completely or partially responsible for their income through entrepreneurship, high commission sales or professional practice.

Since new members enter The 1% Club® already skilled and well seasoned in their professions, our job is to take their success and help them capitalize on it - launching them toward their ideal business situation and lifestyle. New members find The 1% Club® a welcome structure to help them pull together all their assets and then stay focused on their most critical goals.

Your 1% Club team meets every 90 days for a full day to strategically think, plan and adjust course so that you can take advantage of the biggest and most profitable opportunities.

The 1% Club® is a simple, solid and very workable approach to getting the most out of yourself and your life.

If you're ready to set a high character, high performance, high impact example.....

Call 1-800-643-9770 for The 1% Club® application and enrollment information or visit our Web site at www.1percentclub.com.

My Every Desire
Thought Stimulators

Travel
- Where would you like to travel?
- What famous hotels would you like to stay in?
- What famous restaurants would you like to enjoy?
- Where would you take an ideal 30-day vacation?
- What is your favorite climate?
- What cultures would you like to experience?
- What different foods would you like to taste?
- Would you like to visit the moon?
- Would you like to travel first class on every flight you take?

Toys
- What luxuries would you like to be surrounded with?
- What stores would you most like to have a $5,000 gift certificate for? What about $10,000?
- What "toys" would you like to own or have access to? (cars, boats, yachts, a jet, electronics, businesses, etc.)
- What new inventions would you like to see in your lifetime?
- What would you like to see in your wardrobe?
- What sort of collecting are you interested in?
- If you had only one store you could shop in with an unlimited amount of money, which one would it be?

Finances
- What would you like your net worth to be when you're 50? 60? 70? 80?
- How much money would you like to donate to charity in your lifetime?
- What types of investments would you like to be able to make?

- How much money would you like to save up for retirement?
- How much money would you like to save for your children's college education?
- How much money would you like to spend on vacations or adventures each year?
- What causes would you like to support?

Home
- Where would you like to have a second or third home?
- What would your ideal kitchen be like?
- Describe your ideal master suite.
- What style of home would you like? What type of decor?
- What other types of amenities would be part of your dream home? (pool, exercise room, aquarium, office or library, large yard, etc.)
- Who would you like to have design your home?
- How many children would you like to have?

Learning
- What foreign languages would you like to learn?
- What types of lessons would you like to take? (cooking, flying, scuba diving, guitar, karate, dancing, hang gliding, etc.)
- How many books do you want to read in the next 50 years?
- What books would you like to read?
- What knowledge would you like to have?
- Would you like to be known as wise?
- Would you appreciate the reputation of being well-read?
- What new things do you want to learn?
- What unique experiences do you want to have?
- What skills would you like to master?

Health & Fitness
- What changes would you like to see in your physical body?
- What foods give you the most energy?
- What sort of diet would help you achieve more of your other goals?
- What minor discomforts, ailments, weaknesses, or inconveniences would you like to be free from?
- Would you like to run a 5 minute mile?
- What are your favorite types of physical exercise?
- Would you like to have your own fitness center?
- Would you like to have a Personal Trainer?

Relationships
- How would you like the important people in your life to respond to you?
- Describe your ideal mate.
- How would you like your family to describe you?
- What would be your dream romantic getaway for you and your spouse?

Social
- What important people would you like to meet?
- What celebrities would you like to meet?
- What sort of new friendships would you like to develop?
- How do you want to be remembered?
- How would you like your reputation to change in the next 5 years?

Career
- What impact do you want to make on your profession?
- What other types of career opportunities would you like to explore?
- Would you like to go into business for yourself?
- Would you rather be working for someone else?
- How could you create an income source from your hobbies or talents?

Adventures

- How many weeks of vacation would you like to have each year?
- Would you like to have an annual month-long sabbatical?
- Would you like to attend the opening of a Broadway show?
- Would you like to throw out the first ball in a World Series?
- What mountains would you like to climb?
- What great sites would you like to photograph?
- Would you like to ride in a submarine?

Community

- What impact do you want to have in your community?
- What role do you want to play in local, state, national, or world politics?
- What cures for diseases would you like to see come about in your lifetime?
- Would you like to teach a Junior Achievement class?

Personal Comfort

- What "good luck" would you like to experience?
- What emotions would you like to experience more often? How often?
- How often would you like to get a massage?
- What would your ideal weekend be like?
- Would you like to simplify your life?
- What could you eliminate from your life that would give you more inner peace?
- What sort of praise would you like to receive on a consistent basis?
- Would you like to have a full time maid? Chef?

Spiritual

- How active would you like to be in your church?
- Would you like to read the Bible from cover to cover?
- Would you like to teach a Sunday School class?
- What will have to happen for you to experience peace of mind?
- How often would you like to meditate?
- Would a daily devotion at a fixed time each day help you grow spiritually?

Personal Development

- What character traits would you like to develop?
- Would you like to become a vegetarian?
- Would you like to write a book?
- What would you like to be remembered for the most?
- What contribution or talent do you have that would serve others, ultimately reaping rewards for yourself?
- What do you want to do, be, have, or become?

John Goddard: A Legendary Achiever

The more he read, the more ideas he got. And those ideas provided the spark that led John to experience more of life than most people ever dream about. But 15-year-old John Goddard did much more than just dream. He wrote a list of life goals that would shape his life and chart his course for decades to come. With his parents' strong encouragement, John became committed to not just being a spectator, but becoming an active participant in the game of life. Below is John Goddard's original 127 lifetime goals, along with a few recent additions. A ✔ indicates accomplishment.

EXPLORE:

✔Nile River

✔Amazon River

✔Congo River

✔Colorado River

Yangtze River, China

Niger River

Orinoco River, Venezuela

✔Rio Coco, Nicaragua

STUDY PRIMITIVE CULTURES IN:

✔The Congo

✔New Guinea

✔Brazil

✔Borneo

✔The Sudan (Nearly buried alive in a sandstorm)

✔Australia

✔Kenya

✔The Philippines

✔Tanganyika (Now Tanzania)

✔Ethiopia

✔Nigeria

✔Alaska

CLIMB:

Mt. Everest

Mt. Aconcagua, Argentina

Mt. McKinley

✔Mt. Hauscaran, Peru

✔Mt. Killimanjaro

✔Mt. Ararat, Turkey

✔Mt. Kenya

Mt. Cook, New Zealand

✔Mt. Popocatepetl, Mexico

✔The Matterhorn

✔Mt. Ranier

✔Mt. Fuji

✔Mt. Vesuvius

✔Mt. Bromo, Java

✔Grand Tetons

✔Mt. Baldy, California

*Reprinted by permission of John Goddard.

Carry out careers in medicine and exploration (Studied pre-med, treats illnesses among primitive tribes)

Visit every country in the world (30 to go)

✔Study Navaho and Hopi Indians

✔Learn to fly a plane

✔Ride horse in Rose Parade

PHOTOGRAPH:

✔Iguacu Falls, Brazil

✔Victoria Falls, Rhodesia (Chased by warthog in the process)

✔Sutherland Falls, New Zealand

✔Yosemite Falls

✔Niagara Falls

✔Retrace travels of Marco Polo and Alexander the Great

EXPLORE UNDERWATER:

✔Corals reefs of Florida

✔Great Barrier Reef, Australia (Photographed a 300-pound clam)

✔Red Sea

✔Fiji Islands

✔The Bahamas

✔Explore Okefenokee Swamp and the Everglades

VISIT

✔North and South Poles

✔Great Wall of China

✔Panama and Suez Canals

✔Easter Island

✔The Galapagos Islands

✔Vatican City (Saw the Pope)

✔The Taj Mahal

✔The Eiffel Tower

✔The Blue Grotto, Capri

✔The Tower of London

✔The Leaning Tower of Pisa

✔The Sacred Well of Chichen-Itza, Mexico

✔Climb Ayers Rock in Australia

Follow River Jordan from Sea of Galilee to Dead Sea

SWIM IN:

✔Lake Victoria

✔Lake Superior

✔Lake Tanganyika

✔Lake Titicaca, S. America

✔Lake Nicaragua

ACCOMPLISH:

✔Become an Eagle Scout

✔Dive in a submarine

✔Land on and take off from an aircraft carrier

✔Fly in a blimp, hot air balloon and glider

✔Ride an elephant, camel, ostrich and bronco

✔Skin dive to 40 feet and hold breath two and a half minutes underwater

✔Catch a ten-pound lobster and a ten-inch abalone

✔Play flute and violin

✔Type 50 words a minute

✔Take a parachute jump

✔Learn water and snow skiing

✔Go on a church mission

Follow the John Muir trail

✔Study native medicines and bring back useful ones

✔Bag camera trophies of elephant, lion, rhino, cheetah, cape buffalo and whale

✔Learn to fence

✔Learn jujitsu

✔Teach a college course

✔Watch a cremation ceremony in Bali

✔Explore depths of the sea

Appear in a Tarzan Movie (He now considers this a boyhood dream)

Own a horse, chimpanzee, cheetah, ocelot and coyote (yet to own a chimp or cheetah)

Become a ham radio operator

✔Build own telescope

✔Write a book (On Nile trip)

✔Publish an article in *National Geographic* Magazine

✔High-jump five feet

✔Broad-jump 15 feet

✔Run a mile in five minutes

✔Weigh 175 pounds stripped (still does)

✔Perform 200 sit-ups and 20 pull-ups

✔Learn French, Spanish, and Arabic

Study dragon lizards on Komodo Island (Boat broke down within 20 miles of Island)

✔Visit birthplace of Grandfather Sorenson in Denmark

✔Visit birthplace of Grandfather Goddard in England

✔Ship aboard a freighter as a seaman

Read the entire *Encyclopedia Britannica* (Has read extensive parts in each volume)

✔Read the Bible from cover to cover

✔Read the works of Shakespeare, Plato, Aristotle, Dickens, Thoreau, Poe, Rousseau, Hemingway, Twain, Burroughs, Conrad, Talmage, Tolstoi, Longfellow, Keats, Bacon, Whittier, and Emerson (Not every work of each)

✔Become familiar with the compositions of Bach, Beethoven, Debussy, Ibert, Mendelssohn, Milhaud, Rimski-Korsakov, Respighi, Rachmaninoff, Stravinsky, Toch, Tschaikovsky, Verdi

✔Become proficient in the use of a plane, motorcycle, tractor, surfboard, rifle, pistol, canoe, microscope, football, basketball, bow and arrow, lariat and boomerang

✔Compose music

✔Play Clair de Lune on the piano

✔Watch fire-walking ceremony (in Bali and Surinam)

✔Milk a poisonous snake (Bitten by diamondback during a photo session)

✔Light a match with .22 rifle

✔Visit a movie studio

✔Climb Cheopes' pyramid

✔Become a member of the Explorers' club and the Adventurers' Club

✔Learn to play polo

✔Travel through the Grand Canyon on foot and by boat

✔Circumnavigate the globe (four times)

Visit the moon ("someday if God wills")

✔Marry and have children (has five children)

Live to see the 21st century

RECENT ACCOMPLISHMENTS

✔Study and film Sepik River tribes in Papua New Guinea (1995)

✔Cross-country skiing on the Grand Mesa of Colorado (1996)

✔Visit the Hermitage in Russia (1996)

✔Drive a dog-sled through the High Sierras (1997)

Excerpts from:
The Talk Yourself Into Success Series

Talk Yourself
Into *Perfect Health*
• I have perfect health!
• I am perfectly nourished!
• I forgive easily!
• I am elated with life!

Talk Yourself
Into *Peak Performance*
• I am responsible!
• I am a learning machine!
• I am bold!
• I am a creative genius!

Talk Yourself
Into *Super Sales Success*
• I love to sell!
• I manage my time perfectly!
• I have fun!
• I listen well!

Talk Yourself
Into *Rejuvenating Sleep*
• I only say I am tired 3 seconds before I nod off!
• I always sleep perfectly!
• I eat a light, low-fat dinner!

Talk Yourself
Into *Blissful, Loving Relationships*
• I love myself and expect the best!
• I am considerate and polite!
• I laugh a lot!

Talk Yourself
Into *Terrific Time Management*
• I am in control!
• I invest time to plan!
• I make quick, positive decisions.

Talk Yourself
Into *Unshakable Faith*
• I trust God!
• My faith is strong!
• I pray for great faith!
• I ask and I receive!

Talk Yourself
Into *Wealth*
• I deserve wealth!
• I attract wealth!
• I allow and accept wealth!
• I am free!

Tommy Newberry has developed the *Talk Yourself Into Success* series of cards, each with 20 or more affirmations to use in your daily self-talk. For a complimentary set, call 800-643-9770, or visit our Web site at www.1percentclub.com.

About the Author

Tommy Newberry, president of Tommy Newberry Coaching Systems, Inc., is the author of the book *366 Days of Wisdom and Inspiration* as well as the audio programs *High Speed Success*, *Getting Results*, *Vital Time*, *The Secret Place*, *Talk Yourself Into Success*, and *Peak Performance for Christ*.

Tommy is also the founder of the 1% Club®, an elite 3-year coaching program for entrepreneurs, business leaders, and high commissioned professionals. This innovative training approach to life management is designed to accelerate the goal achievement of highly successful individuals in all areas of life. With members enrolled from throughout the United States, The 1% Club® has established the standard for 21st century excellence.

Tommy lives in Atlanta with his wife, Kristin, and sons, Ty and Mason.

Please visit our Web site at www.1percentclub.com or call 800-643-9770 for more information about Tommy Newberry.